School Readiness and the
Characteristics of Effective Learning

School Readiness and the Characteristics of Effective Learning

The Essential Guide for Early Years Practitioners

Tamsin Grimmer

Jessica Kingsley *Publishers*
London and Philadelphia

The accompanying PDFs can be downloaded from
www.jkp.com/voucher using the code 4X57qNjW

First published in 2018
by Jessica Kingsley Publishers
73 Collier Street
London N1 9BE, UK
and
400 Market Street, Suite 400
Philadelphia, PA 19106, USA

www.jkp.com

Copyright © Tamsin Grimmer 2018

Front cover image source: iStockphoto®. The cover image is for
illustrative purposes only, and any person featuring is a model.

Library of Congress Cataloging in Publication Data
A CIP catalog record for this book is available from the Library of Congress

British Library Cataloguing in Publication Data
A CIP catalogue record for this book is available from the British Library

ISBN 978 1 78592 175 9
eISBN 978 1 78450 446 5

Printed and bound in the United States

This book is dedicated to the many early years practitioners and YR teachers who work tirelessly to support children in their transition to school.

Contents

Acknowledgements

This book is a result of many professional discussions, conversations with parents and hours of research. I am grateful to so many people for making this possible, but most especially to my mum for her excellent proofreading skills and to Richard Grimmer, Kate Bate and Bronwen Drewery for our professional discussions. I would also like to thank my friends and family for putting up with me during the writing process and allowing me to share stories about their children and Kym Scott for sharing her experience from Finland.

I would particularly like to thank the following schools and settings who assisted me in my research for this book and provided case studies and information:

Bluecoat Nursery

Byfleet and Pyrford Children's Centre

Byfleet Primary school

Chelwood Nursery School

Douglas Valley Nursery school

Fairytales Playgroup

Forres Sandle Manor School

Guildford Nursery School and Children's Centre

Kinderland Nursery

John Donne Primary School

Kingfield Primary

Kingsham School

Little Forest Folk

Maybury Primary

Noah's Ark Creative Learning Centre

Prebendle School

Pyrford C of E Primary

STARS Group

St Mary's C of E Primary

St Thomas Golbourne Primary School

West Byfleet Infant School

I would also like to thank the team at Jessica Kingsley Publishers for their support and encouragement. Most importantly, I would like to thank the children and parents who have assisted me with my research, I cannot name you all individually but you know who you are and without you this book would not have been written.

Introduction

Children's firsts are celebrated around the world. The first smile, the first wave, the first time they crawl, walk, or talk and one hugely celebrated milestone, the first time they go to school.

This book explores the concept of school readiness by unpicking what the term means for children. When we consider the phrase 'school readiness' and its use and misuse in policy and practice, we perhaps open up a can of worms. There are conflicting views over definitions and the term provokes strong feelings. It is my hope that this book will play its part in the debate and ensure that the views of practitioners, parents and most importantly children are taken into account. It will offer parents ideas of how to support children at home prior to starting school, as well as practitioners in settings and schools. It aims to keep children central to the discussion because they are, after all, the ones who will be starting school.

The transition into school for the first time requires children to cope with many changes. They will have hugely different expectations placed upon them, major changes in their daily routine and changes in their learning environment. This necessitates children to have within them the ability to cope with these challenges and display attributes such as self-confidence and resilience to name but two.

Using this book

The first chapter explores the difficulties in defining school readiness and how a holistic approach may better suit the needs of our children. The second chapter examines the various issues that arise when discussing starting school, such as formal verses informal learning, school starting age and so on. The *Early Years Foundation Stage* (EYFS) sets 'the standards for learning, development and care for children from birth to five' in England.[1] It talks about *Characteristics of Effective Learning* (CoEL) or in other words, the personality traits that make a child good at learning (see Chapter 3). I believe that if a child displays these characteristics they will be empowered to cope with all the demands that moving on to school will place upon them. In Chapters 3, 4, 5 and 6 this book unpicks these characteristics in terms of what they look like for children through case studies and cameos and considers how adults in schools and settings can develop these dispositions and attitudes in the children who are in their care. It offers some ideas of how these characteristics can be fostered through positive relationships and enabling environments. In order for children to be ready for school, they need to be curious about the world around them and have the motivation to engage with learning. It is the responsibility of the adult to ensure that they have provided enough to engage the children, but the children will also need to be ready to actively learn through play and exploration and be able to think critically and creatively about the things that they experience. These characteristics are, in my view, the key to a successful start to school and a good foundation to life-long learning.

Chapter 7 considers children who are ready for school and attempts to advocate for them in the absence of their voice in this debate. Chapter 8 provides ideas and case studies outlining how schools can ensure that they are ready for the children they receive each year and Chapter 9 considers how settings help to prepare children for school and how schools and settings can collaborate together for the benefit of the children. Chapter 10 focuses on engaging parents in the process of preparing their children for school and Chapter 11 sums up the issues discussed looking towards the future. I have also included a glossary which explains key words and phrases used throughout the book. These appear in italics at their first occurrence in the text.

At the end of each chapter I have included some reflective practice questions to enable the reader to review and reflect upon the issues covered in that chapter. In Appendices C and D, there are two self-evaluation tools, one aimed at Reception class practitioners and the other aimed at preschool and nursery practitioners. It is my hope that these will be useful aids for developing your practice, so to support further self-evaluation, Appendices B-D are available to download from www.jkp.com/voucher using the code 4X57qNjW. Appendix E lists books aimed at children about starting school or school in general. These were available at the time of writing and while not exhaustive, the list will be a starting point for you to begin to gather resources.

Throughout this book I use the term 'practitioner' to mean an adult who is working directly with the children and supporting their care, learning and development. This could be in a preschool, nursery, school or home setting. There are many different titles that such adults hold, such as early years educator, early years professional, early years teacher, childminder, playworker, teacher, nursery nurse, learning support assistant, teaching assistant, nanny and many more. I sometimes specifically refer to teachers and teaching assistants in a school setting to differentiate between adults working in a Reception class and those working with children prior to this. Throughout the book I use the term parent to include parent, carer and anyone with parental responsibility for the child.

This book discusses school readiness in relation to all children regardless of gender. Throughout the book I use the terms 'child' and 'children' unless referring to a specific case study or unless the gender of the child is relevant to the context. I have used the term 'school readiness' to refer to the stage when a young child first attends Infant or Primary school, usually entering a Reception class as opposed to a preschool or nursery setting, although as this chapter later discusses, this phrase is loaded with deep feeling and sometimes confusion. I believe school readiness to be a misleading term which could be rephrased somewhat, however it is my hope that this book will be a step towards defining what is meant for the sake of the children. Children must remain central to this concept at all times.

Note

1. Department for Education (DfE) (2017) *Statutory Framework for the Early Years Foundation Stage.* Retrieved from www.foundationyears.org.uk/files/2017/03/EYFS_STATUTORY_FRAMEWORK_2017.pdf, on 2 October 2017, p.5.

1

Defining School Readiness

CHAPTER OBJECTIVE

This chapter will discuss the difficulties of defining school readiness, consider some definitions and propose that a holistic view of readiness is necessary for the wellbeing of our children.

Defining school readiness

Whether or not children are ready for school has become one of the most talked about issues at nursery pick up time, however, in the United Kingdom there is no nationally accepted definition of 'school readiness', so what is meant when this phrase is used? There are many perspectives on this. For a child school readiness could mean being emotionally mature enough to leave their main caregiver for the whole day and cope with life in a class with up to 29 other children and only two adults to support them. For a Reception class teacher school readiness may mean a child can take themselves to the toilet unaided, change for PE with little or no support and be ready to participate in class activities. For parents, school readiness could mean that their child can cope with the many demands that school will throw at their child so that they will settle in quickly. School readiness could also refer to children who can sit quietly and listen for a sustained period, or those who can read and write their name. This book explores what early years practitioners, parents and teachers mean when they refer to school readiness and considers how children can be supported through this time of transition.

Many parents talk to their children about being ready for school and try and prepare them in whatever way they can. For some parents, school was not a positive experience and they have not experienced school life since they left in their teens. These parents may feel anxious on their children's behalf about them starting school. It is easy for this anxiety to rub off onto their children. Other parents may have had positive experiences, however, schools and education in general involve a whole new language and jargon to be understood and interpreted. This can be daunting and confusing with many parents feeling uncertain about the expectations that school will place on their children and families.

In their 2013 report, *What Does 'School Ready' Really Mean?* The Professional Association for Childcare and Early Years (PACEY)[1] states that 97 per cent of childcare professionals agreed on a definition that includes:

children who:

- have strong social skills
- can cope emotionally with being separated from their parents
- are relatively independent in their own personal care
- have a curiosity about the world and a desire to learn.

Many of these ideas are incorporated in the Characteristics of Effective Learning (CoEL) and will be explored in more depth in Chapters 3, 4, 5 and 6.

The United States (US) has been discussing school readiness for many years with most states having defined school readiness locally. The US National Association for the Education of Young Children (NAEYC)[2] produced a position statement on this issue in 1995 and has been updating and revising their position since then. They believe that children are influenced in many ways before they enter school and look at school readiness in a holistic way, considering children, families, communities, schools and the early environment that they have grown up in. This is a helpful stance as children do not grow up in isolation. The theorist Urie Bronfenbrenner attempts to explain the interconnectedness of children's lives through his *ecological systems theory*, which was later renamed the *bioecological model*[3] and can be a helpful tool when attempting to study school readiness holistically.

Defining school readiness in this holistic way is reiterated by organisations such as UNICEF[4] who define school readiness as having three dimensions: ready children, ready schools and ready families. They suggest that readiness for school is not the same as readiness for learning as all children are born with the ability to learn and this learning is not confined to school classrooms. Although this is true, I believe looking at school readiness more in terms of learning enables us to keep the focus on the child.

The *Big Hopes, Big Future Project*[5] by Home-Start UK, a charity funded by the Department for Education, suggests that there are four main indicators of school readiness, 'Language and cognitive skills, behavioural adjustment, children's daily living skills and family support'. Language and cognitive skills cover things such as counting to five, recognising their own name and identifying letters of the alphabet, while behavioural adjustment considers children not being easily distracted, not having tantrums or displaying a lack of patience. Children's daily living skills include using a knife and fork and toilet training and lastly, family support considers the wider implications of family life such as punctuality and absence levels with regard to attendance. Although these broad indicators are helpful because they consider the child as a whole, they also imply that some academic skills are beneficial prior to starting school. I disagree, as from my ongoing research for this book and from my own teaching experience as a Reception class teacher, I believe that teachers are not looking for children who have grasped the 3 Rs (these skills can be taught once a child has settled in school and is developmentally ready). They would prefer children to enter school with the dispositions and attitudes in place which encourage them to learn, which for me is all about the CoEL.

As part of my research for this book, I set up an online poll and invited parents and practitioners from both schools and settings to complete what they felt school readiness meant to them. The poll was open for six months and received nearly 900 votes in this time. Almost all respondents believed that school readiness relates to self-care skills, that is, the child being able to take themselves to the toilet, and 9 out of 10 people believed that school readiness is about the ability to socialise. In addition to this, three quarters of respondents believed that school readiness is about self-confidence, listening to instructions, showing curiosity and interest and being able to separate from their parent/carer for a whole day. If I were to fit these areas into the EYFS,[6]

the statutory framework in England, they fall squarely into the CoEL and the *Prime Areas* which, in England, are the foundation upon which other subject areas are built. In my survey, less than one fifth of people believed that school readiness relates to counting to ten and maths skills, and only one in seven that it relates to children reading and writing their own name. Thus from my small sample of people the message is clear – school readiness is not about academic skills.

However, a belief that children need academic skills prior to starting school has been demonstrated over several years through various government policy statements (see Table 1.1). In the government report, *Supporting Families in the Foundation Years*,[7] they talk about the key elements of school readiness as including children who learn to, 'Speak and communicate, to relate to others, to play, explore their own curiosity, and to enjoy learning through their play as well as beginning to read and write and use numbers.' They go on to say that if we do not fully prepare children for school and the transition into school, then we do them a disservice. This places a huge sense of duty on early education providers and introduces a culture of blame, implying that children will be at a disadvantage if settings do not adequately prepare children for school. In my opinion this is unfair and an example of policy-makers' misunderstanding the role of early childhood education and care providers.

Table 1.1 Summary of government policy with reference to school readiness

Policy document	Date	Reference to school readiness
Field Report on The Foundation Years: Preventing poor children becoming poor adults	2010	Reiterates how preschool and home learning environments determine children's readiness for school
Supporting Families in the Foundation Years	2011	Key elements of school readiness include children who learn to speak and communicate, to relate to others, to play, to explore their own curiosity and to enjoy learning through their play, as well as beginning to read and write and use numbers
Allen Report on Early Intervention	2011	Promoted settings to make sure children are school ready at five years old
Independent review of the EYFS by Tickell	2011	'To avoid the more ambiguous and emotive connotations of "school readiness", I (Tickell) have considered it from the perspective of its opposite: school *un*readiness'
Revised EYFS	2011, 2014, 2017	It (EYFS) promotes teaching and learning to ensure children's 'school readiness' and gives children the broad range of knowledge and skills that provide the right foundation for good future progress through school and life
More great childcare	2013	'More great childcare is vital to ensuring we can compete in the global race, by helping parents back to work and readying children for school and, eventually, employment'
Are You Ready? Good Practice in School Readiness, Ofsted report	2014	Highlights the confusion and strong feelings around the topic of school readiness

Big Hopes, Big Future, Home Start Report	2015	Lists four main indicators of school readiness: 'Language and cognitive skills, behavioural adjustment, children's daily living skills and family support'
The Key: State of Education Survey Report	2016	More than 9 in 10 (98%) of school leaders say that a proportion of pupils join their school below the level of school readiness they expect
The Hundred Review, Early Excellence	2017	Found that, 'The contested concepts of "school readiness" and "schoolification" are considered to be responsible for some of the pressures experienced in YR'
Bold Beginnings: The Reception curriculum in a sample of good and outstanding Primary schools, Ofsted report	2017	The whole aim of this report relates to school readiness as it considers the Reception Year and the extent to which it prepares children for Key Stage 1 and beyond

Confusion regarding entering Reception class or Year 1

For many politicians school readiness appears to relate to academic ability when starting school, as demonstrated in the press release in October 2015[8] stating, 'New figures published today reveal more 5-year-olds than ever before are achieving the expected standards in maths and literacy – meaning more children are on the path to success during their first year of school.' This was using statistics gathered from the statutory *Early Years Foundation Stage Profile (EYFSP)* in England, and just a year earlier an *Ofsted* report used the previous years' results to claim that, 'Too many children start school without the range of skills they need.'[9] The EYFSP is a *summative assessment* compiled at the end of the *Reception year (YR)*, thus children have already been at school for a whole year. News articles such as these highlight the confusion that exists relating to school readiness. They refer to starting school although the data is gathered at the end of the child's first year at school. In addition, referring to the areas of Literacy and Mathematics implies that these are needed for a child to be successful in school, although it could be argued that these are skills that can be easily taught once a child is ready to learn.

Using EYFSP data as an indicator of school readiness also questions whether the term school readiness refers to school entry in Reception classes or entry to Year 1. Ofsted[10] has also recognised that there is confusion over this point. The term school readiness has been used to discuss both readiness for school, thinking about the transition to school from an early childhood setting or readiness for Year 1, thinking about the transition from a Reception class to a Year 1 class. These transitions are not the same and necessitate children to have mastered a very different set of skills.

The EYFSP data considers if children have achieved a *Good Level of Development (GLD)*. This indicates if children have achieved the *Early Learning Goals (ELGs)* in the three Prime Areas (Personal, Social and Emotional Development, Physical Development and Communication and Language) and in the *Specific Areas* of Literacy and Mathematics. If children have achieved at least this level, they have achieved a GLD. This is often used as an indicator for school readiness and is the measure that is used when the headlines talk about school readiness. However, the skillset needed for children entering school for the first time, or children achieving a GLD, is very different.

Discussing school readiness in relation to children entering Year 1 in England could be interpreted as undervaluing the incredibly hard work that goes on in Reception classes across the country. In England the statutory EYFS sets the standards for learning development and care for children aged between birth and five years old. It states that it 'promotes teaching and learning to ensure children's "school readiness" and gives children the broad range of knowledge and skills that provide the right foundation for good future progress through school and life'.[11] This implies that the purpose of the EYFS is primarily to prepare children for schooling, rather than to set the foundations needed for them to become effective lifelong learners. I believe that the early years should not be seen as a preparation for the next stage of a child's life, but as intrinsically important. This idea is also implicit within the EYFS as it states, 'A secure, safe and happy childhood is important in its own right',[12] however, by presenting the EYFS as a preparation stage of learning, they have watered down the intrinsic importance of childhood.

Despite these confusions, within the early years sector it is generally accepted that school readiness refers to entry to Reception classes in the UK and for the purposes of this book I interpret school readiness as being about children entering school for the first year of mainstream schooling. In England, this is typically a Reception class in the academic year that children will turn five years old.

In the *State of Education Survey Report 2016*, The Key[13] asked school leaders about school readiness. A huge 98 per cent of school leaders said that a proportion of children joined their school below the level of school readiness they expected and in the Primary phase, 31 per cent of school leaders stated that more than half of new pupils were not school ready. However, this report did not attempt to define school readiness per se; by using the phrase, 'Level of school-readiness expected' they left it open to be interpreted by the school leaders themselves.

The Key also asked school leaders' opinions regarding what the most common reasons were for children not being at the expected level when they entered school and Figure 1.1 shows the reasons shared. Lack of social skills, delayed speech and lack of self-help skills/resilience were recorded as the reasons most likely to be shared by Primary school leaders. These skills are often referred to as 'soft skills' although I would argue that there is nothing 'soft' about them! They are certainly not insurmountable and as a society we should be striving to build this skillset back into our world and value these skills as highly as we do those that are more academic.

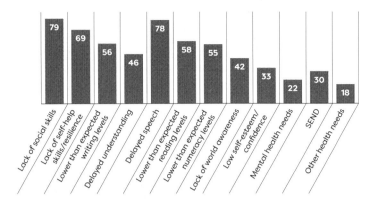

*Figure 1.1 Percentage of leaders' opinions for children
not being at expected level when they start school*

Created using data from the State of Education Survey Report 2016

A holistic view of readiness

If we are to consider children's learning holistically, we need to look at every aspect of their lives, as Figure 1.2 suggests. It includes children having their basic needs met, through positive relationships and enabling environments, demonstrating the CoEL and also having self-confidence, self-esteem, self-care and self-regulation. These elements, for me, allow us to look at school readiness with a broader focus.

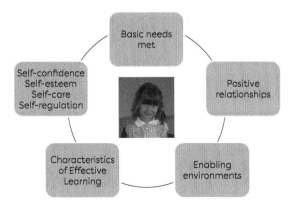

Figure 1.2 A holistic view of school readiness

You may have heard of Maslow's hierarchy of needs, which says that all basic needs have to be met before you can move on to the more higher order needs and wants. This means that basic needs like hydration and nutrition must be considered. Are children coming to school hungry? Have they had enough sleep? Unfortunately some children enter school without their basic needs being met; they may not have had breakfast or a good night's sleep. Children need to be fed and watered and feel refreshed enough before they will be ready to learn. Many schools are aware of these issues and begin the day with breakfast. One school introduced toast and butter to their Reception class straight after they had registered and noticed that the children appeared much more ready to learn during the morning session.

Research has shown that secure attachments are vital in the early years for effective learning to take place. Have we built an atmosphere or fostered an ethos where children feel welcomed, accepted as they are and can build up attachments with us as adults? This is about creating positive relationships with the children and their families in order to support them in the best way that we can. Parents are the children's first educators and Chapter 10 explores some ideas to help practitioners to work in partnership with them.

We also need to consider creating an enabling environment that engages children and motivates them to investigate and explore and has plenty of opportunities for active learning and movement. Reggio Emilia in Northern Italy is highly regarded in terms of its early learning environments. Each preschool centre has a *Pedagogista* (teacher), an *Atelierista* (artist) and they consider the environment to be the third teacher because it has so much to teach the children. The way that we display and store resources will either invite children to play or not. It is important to consider the layout of our rooms: how accessible are the resources for children and how interesting, inviting and stimulating are our environments?

School readiness is also about schools creating this enabling environment so that they are ready to receive the children. This will be explored further in Chapter 8, 'Children-ready schools'.

We also need to ensure that all we do is fostering children's self-confidence and self-esteem so that we are laying the foundations that are necessary to step forward in their learning. Children must have a sense of self-worth and self-belief that they can participate. They need to have some skills relating to self-care, for example being able to take themselves to the toilet on their own. Other self-care skills may still be developing such as using a knife and fork, but it is generally accepted that the more a child can do for themselves the easier they will find the transition into school. Young children are also learning about the process of self-regulation, that is, modifying their behaviour or responding appropriately. We can see this begin in a very young child who may self-soothe by sucking their thumb, for example, if they have been startled by a loud noise. By age four children will be able to anticipate fairly complicated forms of self-regulation, for example, they know that they can clap during show and tell and this is appropriate, however, clapping is not appropriate when the teacher is giving instructions. This is a fairly subtle difference.

When we consider school readiness in a holistic way we are fully supporting each unique child. We are giving them the best possible start to their school life and their ability to become lifelong learners. In his report, written for the Department for Education about early intervention, Allen[14] talks about 'readiness for primary school, readiness for secondary school and readiness for life'. It is the latter phrase that I believe holds most weight. Developmental readiness is perhaps what early childhood educators should be better trained in recognising and supporting and should be the main indicator for school readiness in the UK. In my utopia, there is a flexible school-starting age, where formal schooling starts once children have had lots of opportunities to gain independence and the many dispositions and attitudes that underpin successful adult life. This easily fits into a child-centred pedagogy, which prioritises individualised learning and caters for families as and when their children begin school.

A model for the future

As part of my research for this book, I set up a school readiness research group which included several different schools covering nursery, Reception and Year 1 teachers. We discussed what school readiness meant in terms of the child and developed this model of readiness (see Figure 1.3).

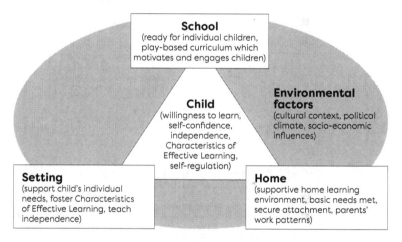

Figure 1.3 Triangle of factors surrounding the child: a model of school readiness

The child is firmly at the centre and around the child there are three main areas of influence: school, setting and home. Each of these areas has key issues that relate to school readiness and support the child. Encompassing all of these areas are environmental factors which can affect the child in a broader context. This is, in our opinion, a comprehensive view of school readiness and hopefully is a helpful model for use when supporting children to transition into school.

When discussing school readiness as part of a professional development course I have developed, I ask delegates to write a recipe for school readiness. So how do we define school readiness and what are the ingredients? In summary, school readiness means many different things to many people, but most importantly, we must ensure that we remember who the recipe is for. Is it to prepare children for the next phase in their education, or is it to equip them for their future lives? Some examples are given below.

School readiness recipe

1 kg – Fun and humour with a hint of cheekiness

2 kg – How to get dressed and go to the loo

5 kg – Good communication skills

1 dollop – Willingness to try and curiosity to learn

4 tbsp. – Following instructions and listening skills

Liberal pinch – Creativity

Sprinkle on – Self-regulation

Mix well and bake between the ages of 4 and 5 and enjoy!

A recipe for school readiness

A cup of curiosity

A tablespoon of self-care skills

A scoop of confidence

1 teaspoon of listening

A cup of communication

1 teaspoon of resilience

An inkling of independence

Mix in some motor skills and sprinkle on some social skills.
Stir it up with a loving arm and exciting environment!

REFLECTIVE PRACTICE QUESTIONS

1. What is your perspective on school readiness and in the absence of any official guidance, could you write your own policy statement owning what it means for you in your setting?

2. Looking at Figure 1.3, which aspects of this model do you have most influence over?

3. What do you believe are the ingredients of school readiness? Write a recipe for school readiness. Think about the ingredients and then add a weighting according to how important you view that ingredient. For example, 1 kg is very important, a sprinkle is not very important.

Notes

1. Professional Association for Childcare and Early Years (PACEY) (2013) *What does 'school ready' really mean?* Retrieved from https://www.pacey.org.uk/Pacey/media/Website-files/school%20ready/School-Ready-Report.pdf, p.1, on 2 October 2017.

2. NAEYC (2009) *Where we stand on school readiness.* Retrieved from https://www.naeyc.org/sites/default/files/globally-shared/downloads/PDFs/resources/position-statements/Readiness.pdf, on 2 October 2017.

3. Rosa, E. and Tudge, J. (2013) 'Urie Bronfenbrenner's theory of human development: Its evolution from ecology to bioecology.' *Journal of Family Theory & Review*, 5(4), 243–258.

4. UNICEF (2012) *School readiness: a conceptual framework.* Retrieved from www.unicef.org/education/files/Chil2Child_ConceptualFramework_FINAL(1).pdf, on 2 October 2017.

5. Home-Start UK (2015) Retrieved from www.activematters.org/uploads/big_hopes_big_future_evaluation_report.pdf, on 2 October 2017.

6. Department for Education (DfE) (2017) *Statutory Framework for the Early Years Foundation Stage.* Retrieved from www.foundationyears.org.uk/files/2017/03/EYFS_STATUTORY_FRAMEWORK_2017.pdf, on 2 October 2017.

7. Department for Education (DfE) (2011) *Supporting families in the foundation years.* Retrieved from https://www.gov.uk/government/uploads/system/uploads/attachment_data/file/184868/DFE-01001-2011_supporting_families_in_the_foundation_years.pdf, on 2 October 2017, p.18.

8. Gyimah, S. and Department for Education (DfE) (2015) *More children than ever starting school ready to learn.* Retrieved from https://www.gov.uk/government/news/more-children-than-ever-starting-school-ready-to-learn, on 2 October 2017.

9. Ofsted (2014) *Are You Ready? Good Practice in School Readiness.* Retrieved from https://www.gov.uk/government/publications/are-you-ready-good-practice-in-school-readiness, on 20 November 2017, p.4.

10. Ofsted (2014).

11. Department for Education (DfE) (2017).

12. Department for Education (DfE) (2017).
13. The Key (2016) *State of Education Survey Report.* Retrieved from www.joomag.com/ magazine/state-of-education-survey-report-2016/0604114001 462451154?short, on 2 October 2017.
14. Allen, G. (2011) *Early Intervention: The Next Steps. An Independent Report to Her Majesty's Government.* London: DfE, p.67.

2

The Starting
School Lottery

CHAPTER OBJECTIVE

This chapter explores how starting school could be compared to a lottery, or a game of chance in terms of school readiness. It discusses issues such as age, country of birth, educational philosophies adopted in that country, and gender.

In recent years, through researching this book and through generally researching early childhood education further, I have found myself more and more convinced that our youngest children deserve to be a higher priority within our modern society. Whilst reading the most recent OECD report,[1] *Starting Strong 2017* I was disappointed, although if I'm honest, not surprised, that England and Scotland come out bottom of 21 countries in terms of the number of hours a week and ages at which children have free access entitlement to pre-primary education. The report also highlights that England is among the countries spending the least on early childhood education and care as a percentage of Gross Domestic Product (GDP). These ideas made me think of the starting school lottery. If you're lucky enough to be born in a certain country, you are a girl and have parents who will support your education, you will transition to school successfully. These issues are explored further in this chapter.

The lottery of formal learning
– a top-down approach

When it comes to early learning and development, there are many different approaches and philosophies that a school or setting can adopt. Many practitioners favour a play-based, child-centred approach which considers the needs of each child and plans appropriate learning opportunities based on their interests and fascinations. Sometimes practitioners feel under pressure from parents, managers, school leaders, committees, Ofsted or even government policy to move to a more formal approach at a younger age. This discourages play-based learning and promotes more traditional methods of teaching, involving children having to sit still and listen for longer periods of time.

When researching this book I noticed that many practitioners, both in early years settings and schools, were concerned about children being pushed into a formal approach too soon. In a nursery setting, this pressure could arise from a parent who asks why their four-year-old cannot yet read independently or from a manager asking how phonics is taught in the preschool room. An experienced practitioner is able to respond by discussing developmental readiness and refer to guidance such as the phase one section within the *Letters and Sounds* document[2] that promotes play-based games to distinguish between sounds as a precursor to formal phonics lessons.

In recent years concerns have been raised in the United Kingdom that preschool teachers are under pressure to ensure that children are school ready. Such concerns have also been recognised in Iceland[3] where children start school at a much older age, yet they are concerned about 'schoolification', when there is pressure placed upon preschools to include more formal school-like learning in their settings, rather than the historically play-based activities that Icelandic pedagogy promotes. This term has also been used by the director of the Pre-school Learning Alliance in the UK to describe what he feels is the top-down pressure being called for by UK government policy and the formal education agenda which prioritises preparing children for school. Neil Leitch[4] states, 'Such "schoolification" is inappropriate for young children and does not take account of their age and stage of development.'

The fact that school readiness features heavily in the introduction to the statutory framework for the EYFS[5] implies that a big part of the rationale behind this document is ensuring that children have the skills needed to start school. It goes on to talk about learning shifting from a more play-based approach to more formal learning as children get ready for Year 1. This implies that adults are encouraging children to be more 'ready' for school through the formal learning experiences that they provide. Moving to a more formal approach has been criticised by Richard House[6] in his controversial book, *Too Much Too Soon? Early Learning and the Erosion of Childhood*, where he argues that pushing cognitive and more formal learning in the early years actually prevents children from learning effectively in the longer term. He shares the term 'toxic childhood' with Sue Palmer[7] who states, 'There is in fact no evidence that an early start to formal education benefits children, and plenty suggesting that a structured child-centred approach breeds more confident, resilient, high-achieving children in the long run.' She believes that the educational system in the UK is led by tests and targets and she is concerned that our government ministers are encouraging schools to introduce children to formal learning at a younger and younger age.

Concerns have also been raised by professionals who see the EYFS as having been 'hijacked' by the narrow agenda of school readiness that is solely preparing children for school perhaps at the expense of more child-initiated experiences.[8] Instead, children should be introduced to more formal knowledge when it is developmentally appropriate for each child. Such an individualised approach, although supported and followed by many early years practitioners nationwide, is difficult to quantify and thus it is very hard to produce measureable outcomes. Unfortunately, in my opinion, it would be unlikely that a government would pursue this approach without a guarantee of data for them to use to measure its success. Early years practitioners must speak out and make our voices heard if we are going to stand up for what we believe is effective pedagogy for young children.

'The first seven years are for play, not school. With time and space to play, children grow up bright, balanced, ready to live and learn with joy and hope.'

Sue Palmer[9] (2016, p.177)

In 2017 Early Excellence conducted a comprehensive review into Reception class practice and views of practitioners working within Reception classes within England. It sought to answer questions related to effective teaching, how good outcomes are achieved and what can prevent or secure progress and attainment in the Reception Year. The review[10] found that, 'The contested concepts of "school readiness" and "schoolification" are considered to be responsible for some of the pressures experienced in YR.' It also talks about the top-down pressure that Reception teachers are under and in the light of this their first recommendation calls on the government to, 'reaffirm its commitment to ensuring that YR remains an integral part of the EYFS',[11] thus safeguarding its status within a play-based curriculum. The Hundred Review also found that although the majority of Reception classes provide opportunities for *child-initiated learning* and adult-directed teaching through *continuous provision*, they find it tricky to ensure there is a balance of both during the day. Reception teachers must safeguard their continuous provision and promote children learning through play and one way of doing this is to use the Characteristics of Effective Learning (CoEL) as a focus for their planning (see Table 2.1).

Table 2.1 Characteristics of Effective Learning – planning

Playing and Exploring – engagement	Active Learning – motivation	Creative Thinking – thinking
I know how to be welcoming and friendly to others	I am developing my confidence to make new friendships and relationships, and work in new situations	I know I have a voice and I know I am listened to
I know how to be friendly to others I am confident with routines and can explain and involve others in them I know what it is to be kind I know how my words can make people feel I know that everyone is valued in our school I can have a go at resolving problems fairly and can seek help if I need it I can welcome other people into my play I can listen to other people and understand what they need I know there are other children who have similar interests to me and some people's interests are different I can help others find their way around	I am confident to work with groups of children I don't usually play with I know I can be friends with lots of people I can share my friends and my friends' time I can share adult time I know how to meet new people and I am learning skills that will help me to make friends I know lots of people can be my friend, at home and school I know that some people can do things that I am still learning to do I can help other children learn to do things I can already to I can share and take turns with others I can play alongside/with others	I can communicate using my voice, words, actions and body language I know my choices and decisions influence others – I can make good choices and help others to make good decisions My family know that I am a capable and independent person and I enjoy learning to do things for myself My family and my teachers talk about how and where I like to learn and the patterns in my play, who I like to play with I'm proud of what I can do, and what I already know I am confident to share and talk with different people about what is important to me, and what I have learnt

cont.

Playing and Exploring – engagement	Active Learning – motivation	Creative Thinking – thinking
I know how to be welcoming and friendly to others	I am developing my confidence to make new friendships and relationships, and work in new situations	I know I have a voice and I know I am listened to
I know when things need to be put back and I know where they belong I can welcome others to explore my classroom I can notice and celebrate differences I am aware of my own emotions and those of other people I can respond to other people's emotions I know that some children are still learning to do things I can already do I can make informed choices that keep me safe, keep others safe and respect things around me I can share and negotiate the space around me I know that I am special and other people are special too I know that not everything involves me and sometimes people need privacy	I know that I am part of a bigger group I can take part in situations that are new to me I am developing the skills and confidence to cope with change I know how to behave to keep myself safe, to keep others safe and respect the environment and I know all adults will help me with this I know how to look after things and where they belong so I can find them I can respond to and value the ideas of others as I play I can respond positively to what people are telling me in their actions and their words	I am able to talk about what I am feeling I know that everyone values my 'Look what I can do!' book and can help me contribute to it I can reflect on how I have changed and what I have learnt to do I know that sometimes it takes time to learn new things I am confident to learn more new things I can use what I know to help me make choices and decisions I can talk to new people about 'what makes me tick' My family know how the staff and learning environment support my learning and development I know that my interests and enthusiasm impact on my learning environment I am confident in sharing my ideas when working in a group I can tell the story of what I'm doing

At the time of writing, the Ofsted report *Bold Beginnings*[12] was published amid controversy within early years circles. This report aimed to provide an insight regarding the extent to which a school's curriculum in YR prepares them for Key Stage 1 and beyond. The report contained various statements which highlighted misunderstandings about how children learn and how YR can be effectively organised and managed through play and child-initiated activities. For example, it highlighted that there is no clear curriculum in Reception and that although play was an important part of the curriculum, schools were not clear about the time they devoted in a typical week to the different areas of learning. This clearly demonstrates a total misunderstanding of Reception, which is in their words, 'a unique and important year' (Ofsted, p.8). If the inspectors had a greater understanding of how children learn in a cross-curricula manner through play, they would not even have asked the question relating to time devoted to different curriculum areas. When play is implemented successfully, different areas of learning and development will be accessed by the child. Take for example a child engaging in mud play within a mud kitchen. They are learning about solids and liquids, changing properties of materials, engaging in physical play, stirring, scooping and spooning the mud. They are expressing the emotions of joy, pleasure and excitement, and their brains are making connections about why things happen and how the world works. As they engage with other children socially, they are interacting with others and using their communication skills. This is not learning taking place during a 'lesson' with aims and objectives relating to one specific area of learning, it occurs during free-play, when the children can initiate their own learning, by accessing what is available to them in the environment through continuous provision. Is this physical development, Personal, Social and Emotional development, Communication and Language, Understanding the World or Maths? All of them! We cannot always compartmentalise learning and shouldn't need to! This is Playing and Exploring, Active Learning and Creating, and Thinking Critically all at the same time. You can imagine the engagement and motivation that mud play provides! This is what effective YR practice looks like.

The lottery of where you were born

Around the world children start school for the first time, but how old you are when you begin formal education depends on where you are born. Despite the compulsory school age in England and Wales being the term after their fifth birthday, the majority of pupils begin school in the September before their fifth birthday and most schools welcome children into a Reception class for a whole year, where children transition into school life. Thus the official starting age is at odds with the actual starting age for most children. In Northern Ireland children also begin compulsory education at age four, making England, Wales and Northern Ireland the countries with the youngest intake of children into Primary education in the world. In Scotland official school starting age is five[13] and children tend to start school at an older age than their English counterparts because children born between March and August start school the following year. In her challenging book, *Upstart*, Sue Palmer[14] makes the case for raising the school age and in doing so explains the political and pedagogical background with regard to starting school. She shares information about other countries and focuses on Finland, a country which is usually in the top five when looking at children's outcomes at all ages. In Finland children begin formal schooling at age seven, have much shorter school days and a much shorter school year than British children, but, they continually outperform our students in all measures. All Finnish children attend a fully play-based kindergarten setting for less than 20 hours per week prior to starting school. Children are valued and education is not viewed in terms of results. One Finnish teacher[15] said, 'School is about finding your happiness, finding a way to learn what makes you happy.'

When we consider international perspectives and school entry ages, we need to ask if the United Kingdom is right in their early school entry age. Using statistics from the World Bank[16] it would appear that in nearly 70 per cent of countries children begin school at age six, just under 20 per cent start school at the older age of seven and half of this number again start school at five or younger. But do British children fare better and gain more qualifications from their early start to school? The short answer is no. In fact, it could be argued that the opposite is true. If we briefly look at the OECD data[17] which outlines qualifications at age 16, the countries that do best in terms of their academic success have an older starting age of either six or seven.

Therefore there is a mismatch between this idea that children attending school at an early age will be higher achievers in the long term; in fact there is evidence from various international studies that support a later start to formal education. A recent Stanford University study[18] considered the mental health benefits when they delayed entry into formal schooling. Professor Dee found that for an average 11-year-old, delaying the start of kindergarten by one year reduced hyperactivity and inattention by 73 per cent. The study used Danish National Birth Cohort data and compared outcomes for children who began formal schooling at age six or delayed until just under seven years old. The study concluded that as older children can better focus their attention, a skill required for school, it is clearly beneficial for children to delay school entry.

Prior to this, in 2002 an American study was published which had followed children through their primary years and correlated their success in school with their school starting age and preschool experience. It concluded that children's success was slowed by introducing formal learning experiences too early and enhanced by a more child-initiated and active learning approach.[19] In the UK, many educationalists have argued that an early start to formal education may be damaging to young children in the long run[20] and the 'Save Childhood Movement' have used evidence such as this to add weight to their recent campaign 'Too much too soon'.[21] They state that one of their main objectives is to, 'Re-establish the early years as a unique stage in its own right and not merely a preparation for school'. They are also campaigning for the EYFS in England to be extended until the end of Key Stage 1 and to be more developmentally appropriate, play-based, informal and rich in learning opportunities.

During May half term Graeme (3 years 10 months) was sitting at the dining table with his two older sisters who were both drawing people. He held a pen in his fist and drew his representation of a person. Graeme had not previously shown any interest in drawing. He carried his picture to his mother and said, 'Look what I've done Mummy!' Graeme is very skilled when it comes to gross motor activities. He loves to ride his bike, can kick a ball and runs and climbs steadily and confidently, however when faced with a fine motor task he struggles. For example, earlier on in the day, when Graeme was putting on his coat and trying to do up the zip, his mother needed to start him off so that he could then pull it up, as fitting one part of the zip into the other presented a difficult challenge for Graeme.

The lottery of when you were born

Graeme is a summer born child; he will be four years old in July and begin in a Reception class just over a month later. He will be one of the youngest children when he starts school in September. This is an example of the lottery of when you are born. In England, we categorise children into *autumn, spring and summer born children*. An autumn born child has their birthday between September and December, a spring born child has their birthday between January and March and a summer born child between April and August. In the past, whether you were autumn, spring or summer born would often determine when you started school according to local arrangements, however, the majority of schools now have a Reception Year which means that all children start school at the beginning of the academic year, albeit sometimes with staggered entry. Thus a child like Graeme can be three years old and start school a couple of months later. Is he likely to be ready to sit down and learn in a formal capacity? I doubt it! Rather, he needs to run, climb, jump, chase, build, race, chatter and play with his friends. This will help him to further develop his motor skills and build his confidence. If a child like Graeme is pushed into formal learning too soon, he will not grasp the joy of learning.

The lottery of your gender

Graeme is at a disadvantage, not just because of his age, but also because of his gender. Generally speaking in child development terms, boys develop slightly slower than girls.[22] There has been lots of debate over the years looking at whether differences in gender are to do with nature (biological differences that we are born with) or nurture (differences that arise due to the influences and gender stereotypes of those around us). In my view this age-old conundrum doesn't need to be an either/or; clearly we are born with some gender differences but also live as part of a gendered society and thus cannot escape the influences of others. It is clear, however, that when we consider early childhood issues boys are at a disadvantage.

As a young practitioner, I was keen to provide gender-neutral colours and toys for the children in my care, yet despite this I still found that the girls tended to be more sedentary, choosing to play with small world toys and 'quieter' activities and the boys would opt for more large-scale construction and chase each other with their home-made guns and lasers! I have learned that many children prefer to play in gendered ways and that this is OK! I can support and extend their play using their interests; however, I am still keen to challenge gender stereotypes and present alternative viewpoints to the children.

The lottery of your individual needs and home background

As Chapter 1 suggested there are various factors that can hinder a child in their learning. The Allen report,[23] mentioned in Chapter 1, highlights the various factors that can influence a child's start in life, for example if they live in social isolation with poor housing or if they did not bond with their mother. Other factors identified as influencing childhood are the socio-economic status of the family and the language that they speak at home. According to the EYFSP data from 2016,[24] *Pupil Premium* children lag behind their peers by 18 percentage points when looking at a Good Level of Development (GLD). Children with *English as an Additional Language* (EAL) are also at a disadvantage, lagging behind by 8 percentage points as accessing school requires a functional level of English. Children also have different levels of need; some may have an identified *Special Educational Need or Disability* (SEND) or health issue that will affect their learning and development, whilst others may struggle with anxiety or have difficulty paying attention. Chapter 7 considers a few of these issues and discusses developmental readiness and the importance of early intervention in order to support children when they start school.

The lottery of parental support

There has been study after study which discusses the importance of parental support and engagement in education and the important difference this makes to children's acheivement. The Effective Pre-school, Primary and Secondary Education research (EPPSE)[25] found that families hold the most influence for children aged between three and sixteen years old. This builds on the Effective Provision of Pre-school Education research (EPPE),[26] which found that what parents and carers do with their young children makes a real difference to the children's development and is more important than their socio-economic status or parent's educational level. So when it comes to school readiness, encouraging parents to engage with their child's learning is a vital component for success. This idea is discussed further in Chapter 10 which looks at parental engagement.

Increasing the odds

Learning happens at all ages and stages of development, and certainly not just at school. To imply that schools are where the real learning takes place is to misunderstand children. We often separate the terms 'learning and development', however, it could be argued that learning is a part of development. If we broaden our thinking around children being ready for school to consider children who are ready to learn, we look at the whole picture, as discussed in Chapter 1.

The various individual circumstances relating to children should not be viewed in isolation. Children, families and schools are affected by the social context and the world around them in many ways. Bronfenbrenner developed his ecological systems theory[27] and bioecological model[28] to explain the layers of influence around a child and the extent to which they are are all interconnected. A child should be viewed in the context of their environment (family circumstances, nursery, local educational systems, community, society) and the relationships between these different groups. Bronfenbrenner would suggest that knowing a child in terms of their temperament and characteristics and investigating the various influences upon their lives will enable practitioners to better understand their children and support them in this starting school lottery.

At some stage, children will venture into this lottery relating to school entry. It is our job as early years practitioners not to leave them to the throw of the dice. We must ensure that we do everything in our power to increase the odds, after all, their childhood is at stake.

REFLECTIVE PRACTICE QUESTIONS

1. How can you ensure that for your children the dice is loaded in their favour in terms of the starting school lottery?

2. What do you consider to be the optimum age for children to start school and why do you think this?

3. Think about the case study regarding Graeme. Is he school ready? What can we do to help him to be more ready for school?

4. If schoolification were a disease, what would be the antidote?

Notes

1. OECD (2017) *Starting Strong 2017: Key OECD Indicators on Early Childhood Education and Care.* Retrieved from www.oecd.org/edu/starting-strong-2017-9789264276116-en.htm, on 5 October 2017.
2. DfES (2007) *Letters and Sounds: Principles and Practice of High Quality Phonics.* Retrieved from https://www.gov.uk/government/uploads/system/uploads/attachment_data/file/190599/Letters_and_Sounds_-_DFES-00281-2007.pdf, on 5 October 2017.
3. Gunnarsdottir, B. (2014) 'From play to school: Are core values of ECEC in Iceland being undermined by schoolification?' *International Journal of Early Years Education,* 22(3), 242–250.

4. Pre-school Learning Alliance (PSLA) (2013) *Alliance concern grows about "schoolification" pressures on early years.* Retrieved from https://www.pre-school.org.uk/alliance-concern-grows-about-%E2%80%9Cschoolification%E2%80%9D-pressures-early-years, on 5 October 2017.
5. Department for Education (DfE) (2017) *Statutory Framework for the Early Years Foundation Stage.* Retrieved from www.foundationyears.org.uk/files/2017/03/EYFS_STATUTORY_FRAMEWORK_2017.pdf, on 5 October 2017.
6. House, R. (2011) *Too Much Too Soon? Early Learning and the Erosion of Childhood.* Stroud: Hawthorn Press.
7. Palmer, S. (2008) *Detoxing Childhood: What Parents Need to Know to Raise Bright, Balanced Children.* London: Orion, p.180.
8. Duffy, B. (2014) 'The Early Years Curriculum.' In G. Pugh and B. Duffy (eds) *Contemporary Issues in the Early Years*, 6th edn. London: Sage.
9. Palmer, S. (2016) *Upstart: The Case for Raising the School Starting Age and Providing What the Under-Sevens Really Need.* Edinburgh: Floris Books.
10. Early Excellence (2017) *Teaching Four and Five Year Olds: The Hundred Review of the Reception Year in England.* Retrieved from http://earlyexcellence.com/hundredreview, on 9 October 2017, p.10.
11. Early Excellence (2017), p.14.
12. Ofsted (2017) *Bold Beginnings: The Reception curriculum in a sample of good and outstanding primary schools.* Retrieved from https://www.gov.uk/government/publications/reception-curriculum-in-good-and-outstanding-primary-schools-bold-beginnings, on 11 December 2017.
13. Scottish Government (2012) *Growing up in Scotland: Early Experiences of Primary School.* Retrieved from www.gov.scot/Resource/0039/00392709.pdf, on 9 October 2017.
14. Palmer (2016).
15. Transcribed from Michael Moore's documentary on Finnish Schools, retrieved from https://www.youtube.com/watch?v=RGR6i0H5ffk at 4.05 minutes.
16. The World Bank (2016) *Official entrance age to primary education (years).* Retrieved from http://data.worldbank.org/indicator/SE.PRM.AGE, on 9 October 2017.
17. OECD (2016) *PISA 2015 Results in Focus.* Retrieved from www.oecd.org/pisa/pisa-2015-results-in-focus.pdf, on 9 October 2017.
18. Wong, M. (2015) Study finds improved self-regulation in kindergartners who wait a year to enrol. *Stanford graduate school of education news center.* Retrieved from https://ed.stanford.edu/news/stanford-gse-research-finds-strong-evidence-mental-health-benefits-delaying-kindergarten, on 9 October 2017.
19. Marcon, R. (2002) 'Moving up the grades: Relationship between preschool model and later school success.' *Early Childhood Research and Practice*, 4(1), 517–530.
20. House, R. (2011) *Too Much, Too Soon? Early Learning and the Erosion of Childhood.* Stroud: Hawthorn Press.
21. Save Childhood Movement, www.savechildhood.net
22. Palmer (2016).
23. Allen, G. (2011) *Early Intervention: The next steps, Report of the Independent Review of Early Intervention.* London: DfE.
24. Department for Education (2016) *Early years foundation stage profile results: 2015 to 2016. Additional tables by pupil characteristics: SFR 50/201.* Retrieved from https://www.gov.uk/government/statistics/early-years-foundation-stage-profile-results-2015-to-2016, on 9 October 2017.
25. Sylva, K., Melhuish, E., Sammons, P., Siraj, I. *et al.* (2014) *Students' educational and developmental outcomes at age 16: Effective Pre-school, Primary and Secondary Education (EPPSE 3-16) Project.* Research Brief. DfE. Retrieved from https://www.gov.uk/government/uploads/system/uploads/attachment_data/file/351499/RB354_-_Students__educational_and_developmental_outcomes_at_age_16_Brief.pdf, on 9 October 2017.

26. Silva, K., Melhuish, E., Sammons, P., Siraj-Blatchford, l. and Taggart, B. (2010) *Early Childhood Matters: Evidence from the Effective Pre-school and Primary Education Project.* Abingdon: Routledge.

27. Bronfenbrenner, U. (1979) *The Ecology of Human Development: Experiments by Nature and Design.* Boston, MA: Harvard University Press.

28. Bronfenbrenner, U. and Ceci, S. (1994) 'Nature-nurture reconceptualized in developmental perspective: A bioecological model.' *Psychological Review,* 101(4), 568–586.

3

The Characteristics of Effective Learning

CHAPTER OBJECTIVE

This chapter will outline the Characteristics of Effective Learning in terms of their historical background, what they mean and examples of what they look like in practice within different contexts.

How young children learn

Young children are learning all the time. From before they are born, their brains make connections as they experience the world using their senses. As children grow they develop certain dispositions and attitudes that can aid their learning, for example, the ability to be resilient and bounce back after experiencing difficulties. If a child develops resilience, they will find it easier to live and function as they grow up.

This is where the Characteristics of Effective Learning (CoEL) come in to play. They are a fundamental tool in understanding how children are making sense of the world around them. They are about **how** children learn, not what they learn, in other words **process** rather than content – how children understand, apply and use knowledge and skills. When children display these characteristics they are making connections in their brain or strengthening *synapses* that already exist.

The CoEL were first introduced to practitioners in England as part of the Early Years Foundation Stage

(EYFS)[1] in 2008 when they formed part of the 4th Principle of learning and development. It talked about children learning through 'play and exploration', 'active learning' and 'creativity and critical thinking'. These characteristics were outlined on three of the principles into practice cards (4.1; 4.2; 4.3). When the EYFS was revised in 2012, 2014 and again in 2017, the characteristics remained with a little wording tweaked here and there.

In planning and guiding children's activities, practitioners must reflect on the different ways that children learn and reflect these in their practice. Three characteristics of effective teaching and learning are:

- playing and exploring – children investigate and experience things, and 'have a go';

- active learning – children concentrate and keep on trying if they encounter difficulties, and enjoy achievements; and

- creating and thinking critically – children have and develop their own ideas, make links between ideas, and develop strategies for doing things.[2]

The non-statutory guidance document *Development Matters*[3] unpicks these characteristics further, offering ideas of what adults can do in terms of building positive relationships and what adults can provide in terms of enabling environments. The three characteristics are expanded under the headings of 'engagement', 'motivation' and 'thinking'. Table 3.1 shows the headings and sub-headings.

I have explored the CoEL in detail in Chapters 4, 5 and 6. It is difficult to discuss one characteristic in isolation, however, for the purposes of this book I have taken each characteristic individually. In the real world, we cannot separate them from each other.

Table 3.1 The Characteristics of Effective Learning

Playing and exploring – engagement	Active learning – motivation	Creating and thinking critically – thinking
Finding out and exploring	Being involved and concentrating	Having their own ideas
Playing with what they know	Keeping trying	Making links
Being willing to have a go	Enjoying achieving what they set out to do	Choosing ways to do things

Although they feature as part of the statutory framework in England, these characteristics generally underpin learning and development across borders and support individual children to be effective, motivated learners. The EYFS itself has been influenced by research, theorists and approaches from around the world[4] and is also shaped by the current political climate.

There is a requirement for teachers to report to parents at the end of the Reception Year on progress in all areas of learning and to Year 1 colleagues on these characteristics. More importantly, in my experience, they can be used as a particularly powerful focus for engaging with parents to gain insights into how children learn in a range of different situations and contexts.

Let's think about what these characteristics look like in relation to children. Playing and exploring is when we see Kate (2 years 11 months) experimenting with gloop – cornflour and water – moving her hands around being totally engaged and having a go, or when Marianna (4 years 2 months) picks up a wooden block and starts using it as a smart phone, swiping it and talking into it. And it's also when Deon (4 years 4 months) goes down the drop slide for the first time, engaging in risky play.

Kate is showing curiosity, engaging in an open-ended activity and using her senses to explore the world around her. Marianna is playing with the concept of phones and using a touch-screen device. She is representing her experiences of smart phones and how she has seen other people use them. Deon is engaging in risky play and trying a new experience which is challenging for him. This is playing and exploring in practice.

Active learning can also be clearly seen in children's play. It's that moment when Isla, an eight-month-old baby, lies on the floor and tries to clasp a toy just out of reach; she tries to reach it for a long period of time and eventually manages to grab it and bring it to her mouth, clearly very pleased that she was successful in her endeavours. Active learning is also illustrated when Bailey (4 years 3 months) decided to make a rocket out of recycled materials (see Chapter 5). He was very focused and was incredibly proud of his rocket, deciding to take it home for his father for Father's Day.

Isla is persevering and maintaining her focus on the desired toy for an extended period of time; she is not easily distracted from her task and displays high levels of involvement. Bailey is also not easily distracted from the challenge he has set himself of building the rocket. He is persistent in his learning and certainly enjoyed achieving what he set out to do. This is active learning in practice.

An example of a child who is creating and thinking critically could be Amina (3 years 7 months) who has recently learned all about shapes and she now sees shapes everywhere – she notices the window is a rectangle and even found an oval on the back of the plastic chair! We can also recognise what children are thinking by what they say. For example Mohammed (4 years 8 months) said, 'My heart is breaking!' after some vigorous exercise which shows that he is thinking about how his heart feels, pumping in his chest. It's also about children like Irena (3 years 4 months) who is problem solving and investigating what happens when water sinks into the earth in the garden (see Chapter 6).

Amina is noticing patterns in her experience and making links between the shapes she has learned about and the shapes in the environment around her. Mohammed is also making links with the language he has heard about hearts breaking and the feeling of his heart pounding that he has after exercise. He is developing his own ideas about how his body works and becoming a thinker. Irena is finding ways to solve problems and investigating and developing her ideas about the world around her. She tests her ideas about water disappearing through holes in the ground by repeating the activity again and again. This is creating and thinking critically in practice.

Effective learning

When we consider the CoEL, we want children to be successful learners and effective in their learning. Young children generally find it easy to learn as they are introduced to new experiences and being taught about things that they previously knew very little about, often on a daily basis. Being effective suggests that we don't just want children to learn; we want them to learn successfully and ensure that they do not have any difficulties or barriers to learning.

Therefore effective learning is about engaging children, interesting them in what we are teaching and motivated them to learn. It can involve:

- Other people
- Objects
- Ideas
- Events
- Time
- Mental engagement
- Physical engagement.

To be mentally or physically engaged in learning, children need to feel at ease, secure and confident. Active learning occurs when children are keen to learn and are interested in finding things out for themselves. When children are actively involved in learning they gain a sense of satisfaction from their explorations and investigations. When children engage with people, materials, objects, ideas or events they test things out and solve problems. The role of the adult is to challenge and extend their thinking and to ensure that they have the time for sustained play and exploration.

Involving children in their learning

We can also involve children in thinking about their learning. Many schools and settings encourage children to talk in terms of learning and one Reception class used dinosaurs to introduce the characteristics to the children.

They talked to the children in terms of explore, try and think and when they posed a problem in class, encouraged them to decide which dinosaur might help them to solve the problem. For example, when the children discovered a leak in the sink area, they needed to use 'thinkosaurus' to solve the problem. They decided that it could be dangerous to allow water to remain on the floor and so, with the teacher acting as scribe, they designed a sign to warn other people not to go into that area. This is children being successful learners and applying their learning to the real world.

Decision-making

For children to learn effectively and be successful, they need to have some independence and control over their learning to keep their interest and to develop their creativity. There needs to be a high probability of success so that children can achieve what they set out to do. This means that we need to plan activities based on what children can already do, with a small amount of challenge or risk to ensure that they stretch themselves. As a basic rule of thumb, think 80 per cent can do, 20 per cent challenge. As children become absorbed in finding out about the world through their explorations, investigations and questions and become successful in their learning, they feel a sense of achievement and their self-esteem and confidence increase. As children grow in confidence it helps them to make decisions based on thinking things through in a logical way.

Personalised learning

Personalised learning involves planning for each child, rather than the whole group. It should also involve parents in their child's development and learning. Begin to plan for personalised learning by knowing about each child's wellbeing. Look at children's involvement in their learning as well as at the nature and quality of adult interactions in children's learning. There are many tools available to support us in measuring children's involvement and The Leuven scale for wellbeing and involvement[5] provides a five point scale for the child's state of wellbeing and a different one for how involved the child is in their activities. It can be a really useful way of evaluating children's engagement. Although occasionally when a child is highly focused their wellbeing may dip, for example when they are concentrating really hard or finding something difficult, for the majority of the time we are aiming for high levels of wellbeing and involvement.

If children are displaying the CoEL and have high levels of wellbeing and involvement, they will be well on the way to being ready for school. These characteristics are like a key to unlocking school readiness. For example, one of the elements of playing and exploring is 'being willing to have a go'. If children are willing, they have a positive disposition and attitude towards learning.

Sinai (3 years 5 months) was brought up in a family whose staple diet was noodles and rice with vegetables, meat and fish. During a session at her preschool after reading the story Handa's Surprise[6] the practitioners brought in a variety of different fruits from around the world for the children to try. Sinai had not seen many of these fruits before but she was willing to try them. She tried guava, mango, grapefruit and fig. Sinai said, 'I like this one because it is sweet (guava)'. Sinai's key person shared this observation with her parents and they replied that they had seen Sinai keen to try all of the different play equipment when she visited a new playground and had had a go on a climbing frame which was unlike any she had ever encountered before.

Sinai was willing to have a go at trying the different fruits even though several of her peers did not want to. This attitude was confirmed by her parents who shared that she demonstrated willingness to have a go on a new climbing frame. Sinai was demonstrating elements of playing and exploring, active learning and creating and thinking critically. She was ready for learning.

Marie (3 years 7 months) wanted to make herself a sandwich. She stood on a step so that she could reach the kitchen worktop and she and her parent discussed what ingredients she would need and ensured that she had them all ready. Marie spread some bread with margarine and cut herself a chunk of cheese to use as the filling. She was proud of her achievement and took great pleasure in eating it for lunch!

Marie is being independent and enjoying making herself a sandwich. She is using her hand-eye coordination and manipulative skills to spread the margarine. Marie was also demonstrating elements of playing and exploring, active learning and creating and thinking critically. She was ready for learning.

Factors that may hinder learning

Children should be supported and encouraged in developmentally appropriate ways and educators must acknowledge that sometimes there are individual circumstances that may affect children's learning. In Chapter 1 we considered how if a child's basic needs are not met, this can hinder their learning. In the same way, if children find themselves in family circumstances that are unsettling, this can also affect their ability to learn.

Family issues such as a new baby, divorce, separation, bereavement, moving house, to name a few, can arise during a child's time attending our settings. Children will be affected by these and other home-based issues and we could be forgiven for thinking that such issues are out of our control as they stem from the home. However, we must remember that we are always in control of how we respond to situations and how we support the children and families involved. For example, if a child's parents are separating, this can be a confusing and upsetting time for the child. We are able to support the child by offering stability and security for them at a time when their home life may lack this. We could share stories with the children which may help them to explore their feelings. We can also gather contact details for both parents, supporting them and remaining flexible in our approach, ensuring that we are impartial in any dispute.

Likewise, if one of the children we care for is about to become an older brother or sister, we can support the child through this time of transition. This is a little easier in terms of supporting the child, since we will know in advance and can therefore help to prepare the child, using stories and discussion. We can introduce role play with babies and maybe even turn the home corner into a baby clinic. Once the parent has had the baby, we can invite them in to share their celebration and encourage the sibling to 'show off' their new brother or sister. However, we need to be aware of the language that we use, as one parent shared with me how they had tried to prepare their four-year-old daughter for becoming a big sister. They kept referring to the baby as 'your baby' and when eventually the day came and they welcomed the new arrival into the world, the four-year-old told the baby, 'I'm your new mummy!' and asked 'When can I keep my baby?' She had thought that the new baby would be hers, a real-life doll for her to look after and exclusively play with! She had quite a shock when she found out she was not, in fact, the mummy!

There may also be in-setting issues that affect a child's learning, for example, if their key person is away or if the routine changes. We need to be aware of how issues within the setting can also affect the children. We may primarily see staffing changes as a management issue; however, children also need to be supported with such things. We can develop a system of buddy key people, so that a second member of staff gets to know the child really well, and if their key person is away, they can step into their shoes and fulfil the role easily. We can also keep children informed of changes to the routine or timings of the day as and when they happen. Many settings choose to use a visual timetable which shows the children in pictures what will happen now and next – see Figure 3.1 for an example.

Snack ➡ Cooking ➡ Story ➡ Home

Figure 3.1 A visual timetable

The CoEL are explored in more detail over the next few chapters, however they summarise the various dispositions and attitudes that most practitioners would want their children to achieve, not only in the early years, but throughout their lives. This is, in my opinion, the practical application of school readiness.

REFLECTIVE PRACTICE QUESTIONS

1. How do you involve children in their learning?

2. What factors may be hindering the learning of the children in your setting?

3. How do you foster the CoEL in your children?

Notes

1. Department for Children, Schools and Families (DCSF) (2008) *The Early Years Foundation Stage.* Retrieved from www.foundationyears.org.uk/files/2011/10/ EYFS_Practice_Guide1.pdf, on 9 October 2017.
2. Department for Education (DfE) (2017) *Statutory Framework for the Early Years Foundation Stage.* Retrieved from https://www.foundationyears.org.uk/ files/2017/03/EYFS_STATUTORY_FRAMEWORK_2017.pdf, on 9 October 2017, p.10.
3. Early Education (2012) *Development Matters in the Early Years Foundation Stage.* London: Early Education.
4. Wall, S., Litjens, I. and Taguma, M. (2015) *Pedagogy in Early Childhood Education and Care (ECEC): An International Comparative Study of Approaches and Policies Research Brief.* Department for Education. Retrieved from https://www.gov.uk/ government/publications/early-years-pedagogy-and-policy-an-international-study, on 9 October 2017.
5. Laevers, F. (2005) *Sics (Ziko) Manual Well-being and Involvement in Care: A Process-oriented Self-evaluation Instrument for Care Settings.* Leuven, Belgium:Kind & Gezin and Research Centre for Experientel Education. Retrieved from https://www. kindengezin.be/img/sics-ziko-manual.pdf, on 9 October 2017.
6. Brown, E. (1994) *Handa's Surprise.* London: Walker Books.

4

Playing and Exploring

CHAPTER OBJECTIVE

This chapter will unpick playing and exploring, relate it to children and consider how these skills map upwards into school whilst also considering practical ways of supporting children through creating enabling environments and promoting positive relationships.

Have you come across the phrase, 'Time flies when you're having fun?' I have found this to be so true; when I am fully absorbed in a good book, or watching a film or play, it is as if the real world around me is diminished to the shadows and I am transported into the scene I am engrossed in. According to Alan Watts,[1] this level of engagement is the real secret to life and it is this deep level of involvement and engagement that children regularly achieve when they are playing and exploring. Imagine a child so immersed in their play that they enter their own play world and they are not easily distracted out of it.

This type of engagement with activities often arises when children freely choose what to do, which is usually during free-play or self-chosen activity time. The guidance document *Development Matters*[2] unpicks playing and exploring in terms of engagement and as having three elements: finding out and exploring, playing with what they know and being willing to 'have a go'. This chapter will consider these aspects, including what they look like in practice and how adults can further support children.

The following case studies have been interpreted in the light of playing and exploring, however, many of them could easily link to other characteristics.

Kate (2 years 11 months) is standing next to the builder's tray which is filled with gloop (cornflour and water). She uses both hands to swirl the gloop around in circular motions and then carefully uses her index finger to make various marks in the tray.

James (3 years 7 months) is at the sand tray. He fills an old coffee tin with dry sand using a scoop and tips it out. The dry sand collapses into a pile. James looks up at the practitioner, 'It's disappeared!' He looks and thinks for a while, then says, 'Oh no, I can't make a sandcastle. I need you to help me.' The practitioner and James talk about what could help to make the sandcastle and the adult provides some water in a bowl for James to use. He tips the water into the tin and then scoops some sand into it. He stirs the mixture for some time, and appeared fascinated by the bubbles forming on the surface of the mixture. He then eventually tips the tin upside down, but the sand sticks in the tin. James spends more time finding ways of getting the sand out of the tin.

Ella (3 years 10 months) was in the outside area near the tool bench. She was watching some other children using the tools. Ella picked up a hammer and wanted to hammer some wood. She carried it to her key person saying, 'Can you help me hammer?' Her key person explained that she needed a nail to hammer into the wood and she showed Ella where to the nails were kept and then offered to hold the wood still while Ella used the hammer. Ella tried to hold the nail with one hand and the hammer in the other hand, but found this tricky. Her key person helped her to start off the process and once the nail was secure, Ella used both hands to hold the hammer.

Mariana (4 years 2 months) was in the role play area with a wooden block in her hand. She said, 'This is my phone, I take it to work.' She used her left hand to hold the block and the index finger on her right hand to swipe at the 'touchpad' on the block. She then put it into a handbag with some paper and walked off saying, 'Ciao, ciao!'

When his nursery visited a farm park, Deon (4 years 4 months) was particularly awestruck by the drop slide. He had never seen one before and he slid down it repeatedly. He told his key person that he loved it because it made him feel like he could fly!

Finding out and exploring

This element of playing and exploring is about children showing curiosity. Think about a child who is curious about different objects. They often ask lots of questions. What is it? What does it do? Can I touch it? They often want to explore objects using their senses and will most definitely want to touch things that they see. Imagine every parent's nightmare, when they go into a gift shop with young children, trying to encourage children to look only using their eyes. This is difficult for most young children as they 'look' with their hands too.

Children use their senses all the time to explore the world around them and using their senses will reinforce the synaptic connections in their brain. Practitioners need to encourage this sensory exploration by providing many different experiences which can be explored in different ways. Finding out and exploring is all about hands on learning, getting your hands dirty – literally, just like Kate did!

James was showing curiosity about materials and was interested in the differences between wet sand and dry sand. He was engaged in this open-ended activity. He clearly started out by wanting to make a sandcastle but his desire to create the castle was soon overwhelmed by his desire to explore the sand and water mixture. Ella demonstrated her interest in using the tools and wanted to challenge herself by hammering a nail.

When children show particular interests and fascinations they are also finding out and exploring. We can encourage children to develop their interests and observe children carefully so that we can recognise when they are showing a particular interest in something. If we tap into these interests we can ensure that we provide resources that are relevant to them. This will help to engage our children further. For example, observing Deon could provide evidence of *schematic behaviour*[3] as he was participating in activities associated with the trajectory schema. We can provide additional activities that link with trajectory movements to enhance his learning.

Playing and exploring is also about engaging in open-ended activities because children are able to learn much more through these activities. Most people have come across using open-ended questions to engage children in learning – questions that have many possibilities rather than one specific answer. Like questions, an open-ended activity would have many different possibilities.

OPEN-ENDED ACTIVITY

Imagine this scenario:

Thomas (4 years 6 months) was at his grandparents' house for the weekend. Thomas told his grandparents that he wanted to build a den and they agreed that this was a lovely idea. He carefully put the garden chairs apart, then borrowed a large sheet from his Granny and placed it over the garden chairs. Unfortunately the sheet kept slipping off the chairs which caused quite a discussion. Thomas asked if he could attach the sheet using tape, however his Granny was not so keen on this idea. They eventually decided to use clothes pegs and Thomas carefully pegged the sheet over the chairs. Thomas then spent a long time arranging the inside of the den with cushions and a rug. He asked if he could have his snack in the den and ended up playing in the den for most of the morning. Creating the den involved lots of discussion, problem solving and creative thinking.

CLOSED ACTIVITY

Now compare that with this scenario:

Thomas was at his grandparents' house for the weekend. Thomas told his grandparents that he

wanted to build a den and they agreed that this
was a lovely idea. They provided him with a pop-up
tent which Thomas and his granny erected in three
minutes. Thomas played in the den for a couple
of minutes and then wanted to do something else.

When Thomas was provided with the materials with no
fixed method of how to create the den, he was able to play
and explore and find out. His Granny did not take over the
activity, she just presented him with options and supported
his ideas. When the sheet slipped off the chairs, Thomas
was learning through trial and error and problem solving to
find a way of attaching the sheet securely. The open-ended
activity captured Thomas's interest and engaged him in play
for a lot longer than the closed activity. The pop-up tent did
not require Thomas to problem solve or be creative and,
although it created a similar play space, Thomas quickly
became bored and this play did not fully engage him.

Playing with what they know

This element is about children using their knowledge and
understanding about the world and applying it to their
play. James is playing with what he knows by using his past
experience of making a sandcastle. He knows how to fill a
container with sand, turn it upside down and make a castle,
however his first attempt with fully dry sand didn't work!
This opened a door for him to explore the properties of wet
versus dry sand and tapped into his interest in mixing and
transforming materials.

Mariana is taking on a role in her play as she imagines
she is working in an office. She has seen other people using
touch-screen devices and 'created' her own using a wooden
block. She demonstrates her competence in swiping the
screen and in doing so is using her imagination and
representing her own experiences in her play. We all draw
on our own first hand experiences in life and children are

no different. They will make links in their experiences, play with ideas and concepts and engage in pretend play on a variety of levels.

TOP 5 WAYS TO PROMOTE A 'CAN DO' ATTITUDE

1. Provide children with open-ended activities and resources that have no 'correct' answer and many different outcomes.

2. Share stories about characters who have taken a risk, engaged in new experiences or demonstrated a 'can do' attitude.

3. Create an 'I can do!' notice board with photos and learning stories celebrating children's achievements and share successes with parents and carers.

4. Allow children to make choices, develop ideas and be responsible for specific tasks, e.g. setting the table for lunch or looking after a younger child.

5. Model getting things wrong and encourage the children to help you to problem solve and find a solution.

Being willing to have a go

At the heart of playing and exploring is the 'can do' attitude and children being willing to have a go. This attitude defines those who are successful in life. As an adult, my life is enriched by being willing to engage, try new things, visit new places and have a go, although this is a concept that many people, including adults, find very difficult. It involves change, risk and challenge and, although easy to say, can be very difficult to undertake.

Chapter 7 further considers how we can support children with change in the context of starting school, which is a new experience for most children. Such experiences can be challenging because they involve trying new things. Deon was confident to try the new slide and obviously enjoyed it. Having a go like Deon is a great attitude to foster, however it comes hand in hand with risk. What if I don't like it? What happens if I'm scared? Is it safe? How will I get back down if I don't want to use the slide? Ella and Thomas both initiated their own learning in different ways. Thomas demonstrated a 'can do' attitude as he built the den with his Granny. Ella chose to try something new and take a risk by engaging in a challenging activity. She needed to be careful using the hammer and the level of risk will have increased her concentration tenfold!

Learning through trial and error could also be seen as risk taking. Is it OK to get things wrong? How will I feel? How will the adults react? Will I be allowed another attempt? James was engaging in an activity that he chose and was also learning through trial and error. He asked for help when needed and, despite the challenges that he met during his play, James was keen to persist and maintained focus on this activity for a long period of time.

Learning in this way could also be described as learning from your mistakes, which is often seen as a life skill and way to develop character, so much so that Cheryl Cole has been quoted as saying, 'I've learned so much from my mistakes...I'm thinking of making some more!' Children need to learn that it's OK to make mistakes and this is what we do about it: we get up, brush ourselves down and try again. It can be helpful if as practitioners, we sometimes openly make a mistake, spill the milk for example, and then show the children how we respond. 'Oh dear! I've spilled the milk! Never mind, I just need to get some paper towels and wipe it up.' Then we can talk through the process of cleaning up and pour ourselves another cup of milk to show that everything is OK. Some children grow up in homes where it is not OK to spill the milk, so let's ensure that our early years settings are places where children can grow and learn through childlike blunders.

Playing and exploring – an element of school readiness

The case studies discussed in this chapter are about children who have engaged in the characteristic playing and exploring and who are, in my view, ready for school. If children are showing curiosity, engaging in open-ended activities, using what they know about the world in their play and being willing to have a go, take a risk and challenge themselves, they will soar at school.

Most Reception classes will require children to fit in with the rules and expectations of their school which may differ from those of their early years setting or home. If children demonstrate a 'can do' attitude it will stand them in good stead as they will be required to try new activities on a daily basis and if they are curious learners they will be happier to engage in these. Starting school will also require children to take risks such as talking to a new person and this can be frightening. What shall I say? What if they don't like me? Will they be my friend?

As practitioners we must work hard to ensure that play and exploration is given the priority it deserves in our busy schedules and this will, in turn, assist with school readiness.

The role of the adult in supporting playing and exploring

Adults need to provide a rich, stimulating environment with plenty of opportunities for exploration, discovery and fun. We set up invitations for children to learn and spaces where they can initiate their own ideas. Jan Dubiel[4] describes children who engage in self-initiated play as those who, 'make sense of the knowledge and skills that they have by taking what they know, or have been taught, and applying it to their own interests, driven by their own motivations and immersed in their own fascinations'.

This is about adults tuning in to children and our role is sometimes just to stand back and be observers or listeners. This way we discover just how much the children know about the world around them and about different occupations and experiences. By knowing the unique children in our care and understanding their likes, dislikes, interests and strengths we are able to create and foster an environment where they will soar. So we can use our observations to plan future learning opportunities and adapt and *differentiate* our provision to meet the individual needs of the children in our care.

We can support children to play and explore by ensuring that all areas of learning and development are delivered through play-based activities with plenty of open-ended opportunities with which they can engage. Planning a mixture of adult-directed tasks alongside time for children to initiate their own learning is essential. Sometimes children may need to be shown how to use equipment or taught key skills before they are able to access the resources independently. However, we will still want to ensure that there is adequate time for children to play and explore in depth and really become engrossed in learning.

Part of our role is to plan an effective and challenging learning environment so that play can happen spontaneously and independently whilst introducing elements of challenge and risk. We can act as a role model, demonstrating to children how to investigate and take risks. In addition, we must ensure that tools, equipment and resources are accessible and clearly labelled for children to use independently.

We will also make sure that there is an ethos of permission for children to play and explore. We can do this by talking to the children about which spaces they can play within, which resources they can use and how they can use them. I was once undertaking some consultancy in a school where children were not using their creative area independently, although they were able to access the resources and space easily. I spoke to several children who explained that they weren't allowed to use the space. This was not, in fact, the case as they had never been told this. The children were under the impression that they were not allowed to use the area as all of the resources were in drawers neatly labelled whereas other areas of the setting resources were on table tops or in boxes on the floor. Once children were shown how to pull open a drawer and use the resources, the space was freely used.

We can also support children to play and explore by providing exciting resources and materials that encourage children to role play, use their imagination and represent their ideas and experiences. Large pieces of material lend themselves to becoming anything from a cloak or superhero cape to a den covering or tablecloth. In addition, large blocks and boxes can foster children's creativity and encourage them to design and build their own creations. There is also a place for specific props and resources which can support children's role play, for example, builders' hard hats for a construction site or superhero masks to enhance imaginative play. Some settings invite the children to plan parts of the learning environment with practitioners and make resources and props together to enhance their small world play, role play area or home corner.

ASSESSMENT OPPORTUNITIES

When assessing children's learning consider:

Finding out and exploring

- What areas/activities are they drawn to?

- Do they prefer to work in a group/alone?

- Do they engage in open-ended activities?

- Do they initiate activities themselves or join in an existing one with a group?

- Do they think aloud, describing what they do?

Playing with what they know

- In play do they draw on experiences from home/ outside school?

- Do they act out situations in the role play area?

- Are they confident in finding tools, materials and resources they need for a particular project or idea?

Being willing to 'have a go'

- Do they initiate their own activities and seek challenge?

- Levels of persistence – do they give up at first hurdle or keep trying?

- Are they eager to try new ideas or do they stay with what they are familiar with?

- Are they able to talk about/review what they've done if things haven't worked?

- Do they work best with continual support or prefer to get on with activities themselves?

(Adapted from Jan Dubiel[5])

When we offer children opportunities to investigate, use their senses and engage in open-ended activities, they will be playing and exploring. We can foster a 'can do' attitude through our positive relationships and the enabling environments that we provide. These ingredients will ensure that children are fully engaged in learning, which will help to prepare them for school.

REFLECTIVE PRACTICE QUESTIONS

1. What opportunities are there for children to play and explore in your setting?

2. How do you know when children are fully engaged in learning?

3. How might you foster a 'can do' attitude in the children in your care?

4. What opportunities are there for children to take risks and engage in challenging activities?

Notes

1. Watts, A. (1977) *The Essence of Alan Watts.* Berkeley, CA: Celestial Arts.
2. Early Education (2012) *Development Matters in the Early Years Foundation Stage.* London: Early Education.
3. Grimmer, T. (2017) *Observing and Developing Schematic Behaviour in Young Children: A Professional's Guide for Supporting Children's Learning, Play and Development.* London: Jessica Kingsley Publishers.
4. Dubiel, J. (2012) 'Learning and Development: How Children Learn: Part 1 – In the process.' *Nursery World,* 3 February, 2012.
5. Dubiel (2012).

5

Active Learning

CHAPTER OBJECTIVE

This chapter will consider active learning and share case studies about children learning in this way. It will also consider practical ways of supporting active learning within the context of children preparing for school.

Spend a moment or two thinking about what motivates you. What really gets you going? I am motivated when I am doing something that I enjoy, or participating in something where I am making a difference. I am also motivated by learning new things; for example, I am enjoying the process of writing this book. If my motivation were purely to see the end product, a book on a shelf, I may find the journey rather tiresome. This is the difference between *intrinsic and extrinsic motivation*. Doing something because you enjoy the process and want to do it for its own sake is an example of intrinsic motivation. Doing something purely for a reward or benefit is an example of extrinsic motivation. The most powerful motivator is intrinsic; it comes from within the learner.

Motivation is also important with children. As Nicola Call and Sally Featherstone[1] state, 'The intrinsic motivation to learn is one of the greatest tools that a child can have.' Do children want to engage in the activities and learning environment that we offer them because they enjoy it or are they complying with our needs and wishes purely to get a 'well done' or sticker at the end of the day? We need to find out what motivates our children and use this information to plan an interesting, exciting and stimulating environment, one which they can't wait to dive into.

The guidance document *Development Matters*[2] unpicks active learning in terms of motivation and as having three elements; being involved and concentrating, keeping on trying, and enjoying achieving what they set out to do. This chapter considers these elements and shares some case studies of children who are demonstrating this characteristic. For the purposes of this section, 1 am focusing on active learning, however many of these case studies would also demonstrate the other Characteristics of Effective Learning (CoEL) as it is difficult to isolate these aspects of learning.

Isla (8 months old) is lying on her tummy on the play mat. She lifts her head, pushes on her arms and arches her back to hold herself up. Isla reaches for a rattle that is just beyond her grasp. She looks at it and then reaches her right arm towards the rattle. Isla persistently reaches again and again and as she does so her body inches towards the rattle. Eventually Isla manages to grasp the rattle. She brings it to her mouth and looks very pleased that she managed to grab it.

Bailey (4 years 3 months) created a rocket out of a cardboard box, egg box and bubble wrap. When

Bailey was attaching the blue card to make the rocket's apex, the card was difficult to attach. Bailey wanted to use a stapler, but found that he couldn't reach the arm of the stapler through to the point that needed joining. He then tried to use PVA

glue, however the card slipped down before the glue had dried. Bailey decided to use sticky tape and was, at last, successful! He added to his rocket every day over a period of three weeks, painting, gluing on feathers and amending his design to improve it. After several weeks Bailey decided to take his rocket home to give to his father for Father's Day.

Graeme (3 years 10 months) was at the park with his family. He was climbing on the climbing net, shaped like a web. He called to his mother, 'Look at me! I'm higher!' He spent a further 10 minutes climbing around the edge of the net before trying to climb upwards and inwards towards the top. He managed to climb a little way then his older sister started rocking the ropes. Graeme shouted and told her to stop. Once the ropes stopped shaking he continued to climb upwards. He revisited the same park on a number of occasions and after several attempts managed to climb to the top of the web.

Emily (2 years 2 months) was very involved and concentrated for a long time while painting. She used the brush to make marks on the paper. She soon had another idea and tried a different approach, painting her hand. Emily certainly showed great satisfaction and joy at completing this picture!

Skye (4 years 5 months) received a pack of lolly sticks and a pattern of how to make them into a bird box. She carefully followed the picture instructions and assembled the bird box with very little adult help. Skye was not easily distracted from this task and enjoyed making the bird box. She was also very proud of her finished product, showing it off to her brothers when they got home from school. Later, she hung it in the garden for the birds to use.

Being involved and concentrating

Active learning is about children being able to maintain their focus on whatever they are playing with for a sustained period of time. True focused attention is when children are not easily distracted and spend time becoming engrossed in their play, as was discussed in Chapter 4 when considering engagement. This high level of involvement can be seen at a very young age, as demonstrated by baby Isla who is very persistent in reaching for the rattle. She dedicates lots of energy to the task of reaching out and her concentration is clear to see. This dedication to activities will stand her in good stead for school in a few years' time.

Angela Hanscom[3] states, 'In order for children to learn, they need to be able to pay attention. In order to pay attention, we need to let them move.' She argues that children are moving around less and less in modern society and this is having an impact on their ability to concentrate and pay attention. Many recent research studies have shown that children who move around are better able to concentrate and the Department of Health[4] in the UK has recommended that children under five who are capable of walking should engage in physically active play for at least three hours each day. In addition, children's gross motor skills develop prior to their fine motor skills and children need to practise and perfect large movements before they can refine smaller movements.

Graeme is very active as he plays on the web in the park. He stays focused on his idea to climb higher on the web and over a period of time his focused attention pays off and he is successful. Graeme demonstrates high levels of energy when trying to achieve his goal. As we have heard that being physically active can help children to be more focused in the classroom then this time in the park is preparing Graeme for school.

Bailey is also maintaining focus on an activity for a long period of time and like Graeme, he is returning to the same task over several weeks. He pays attention to the detail of his rocket, adding extra feathers and enhancing how it looks. Emily and Skye are also fully involved in their creations, concentrating hard on their tasks.

Keeping on trying

This element of active learning is about perseverance and resilience. Perseverance is the ability to try and try again and resilience is about bouncing back after difficulties. Both skills are useful in life in order to be successful learners. Everyone encounters difficulties to a greater or lesser extent every day and needs to overcome these. However, as *Resilient Therapy*[5] implies, real resilience is demonstrated when a child not only overcomes difficulties but experiences better outcomes than were expected, sometimes even turning adversity into success. In other words, what doesn't kill you makes you stronger!

Even at her young age Isla demonstrated her ability to persevere as she kept trying to reach the rattle that was just out of her grasp. Bailey needed resilience to work through the difficulties that arose when he was trying to connect the card apex onto his rocket. He was persistent and tried different approaches, believing that he would find a solution in the end. Graeme also had to persevere when climbing on the web and he even had to wait until his sister stopped rocking the ropes. It was rather challenging and pushed his climbing skills to the limit. Again, his perseverance paid off when he successfully climbed to the top of the web at a future visit to the park.

TOP 5 WAYS TO PROMOTE PERSEVERANCE AND RESILIENCE

1. Provide children with opportunities to problem solve and engage in activities over a sustained period of time.

2. Share stories about characters who have needed to persevere or demonstrate resilience.

3. Teach children mantras such as 'try and try again' so that they can talk themselves through problems and keep on trying.

4. When planning activities, make sure that they are broken down into smaller achievable steps which allow children to succeed.

5. Role model trying and trying again and bouncing back after difficulties.

Enjoying achieving what they set out to do

The great thing about having perseverance and being resilient is that they often lead to success! Children who demonstrate that they are active learners will be satisfied when they meet their goals and manage to accomplish tasks. This is clearly seen when Isla grasps the rattle and is able to move it to her mouth. She is really pleased to be able to chew on the rattle that she has spent so long trying to reach.

Bailey was really proud of his rocket, so much so that he decided to give it to his father for Father's Day. The joy that Emily feels as she paints is evident in her face, she is certainly enjoying achieving what she set out to do! Skye also demonstrates pride in her creation and wants to show it off to her brothers. She felt that she had really accomplished something, having followed the instructions and built the bird feeder with very little help from an adult. It is this intrinsic motivation that will help children to become active learners.

We can encourage children to share their achievements and accomplishments with each other. Many settings encourage parents to share successes from home too, using systems such as 'proud clouds' or 'stars' which can be displayed and celebrated in the setting. Children love to be praised, however, it is vital that we use praise wisely to encourage children and not to create praise junkies – children who need to get a 'well done' to feel that they have achieved something. Therefore we need to use encouragement strategies rather than straight praise and specifically label any praise we give. For example, when we want to praise a child for doing something, rather than saying, 'Good girl!' or 'Well done!', we could say, 'Great sitting, Jack!' or 'I like the way you have used so many bright colours!' These statements provide the child with feedback about what it is that they have done that is good or being praised.

Active learning – an element of school readiness

The children discussed in this chapter are all demonstrating that they are active learners and on their way to being ready for school. Children will need to be intrinsically motivated to continue their learning journey through the Primary years. One boy in a Reception class, when he was promised a sticker if he completed a task, stated, 'I don't want one anyway. I have loads of stickers at home and can have one whenever

I want.' He had no desire to get a sticker for his efforts, but when the teacher realised that he loved Spiderman, she was able to tap into this interest and plan a task around webs, which he joined in with great enthusiasm.

Play still has a high priority within effective Reception classes and children are encouraged to become independent learners, however, most schools will require children to concentrate on tasks and activities or sit still during an assembly at some point during this first year. As mentioned previously, children need to have moved around a lot in order to be able to sit still and focus. Some schools are allowing children to engage in physically active play before expecting them to sit still for sustained periods of time. Encouraging children to be physically active learners will help them to meet the expectations that school may demand.

Children may also come across difficulties and challenges in school. For example, learning to read takes a lot of effort on the child's part. They will need to want to read and see how reading can benefit their lives. This will require motivation, perseverance and resilience and a child who demonstrates that they are an active learner will be best placed to undertake this task. As practitioners we must ensure that we teach children the skills needed to become active learners.

The role of the adult in supporting active learning

We can foster the characteristic of active learning in our children through positive relationships and enabling environments. We need to ensure that we offer depth not just breadth in activities to allow children to become competent and gain mastery over the skills they are learning. This will require us to plan for sustained periods of time which allow for children to become fully engrossed in their play. Therefore we must provide children with uninterrupted time to play and initiate their own learning.

We may choose to use the Leuven scale for wellbeing and involvement[6] mentioned in Chapter 3 as a way of assessing how involved and engrossed children become in their play, whilst also monitoring their levels of wellbeing. We can use this information to assist us in planning future learning opportunities and improve the mental health of the children in our care.

As adults we need to interact sensitively and effectively without jumping in too soon. This is a difficult call to make as Julie Fisher[7] indicates with the title of her book, *Interacting or Interfering?* So we need to use our knowledge of the children to know when to intervene and extend children's learning or when to remain observing. As mentioned earlier we need to label-praise and use encouragement strategies to inform the children what they have done well and provide them with ideas of how to improve. This also helps to shift away from the 'adult-pleasing culture' which can be prevalent in some schools and settings.

We can also role model behaviours such as perseverance and risk taking and use the language associated with learning so that we are not just directing the children but enabling them. In addition, we can show the children that we also make mistakes and that we can bounce back as this will help to build perseverance.

It is important that we provide children with enough challenges so that that they are really learning and not just coasting. The theorist Vygotsky talks about the *Zone of Proximal Development*[8] which refers to the difference between what children can do independently and what they can do with support. It is in this zone that real learning takes place. We can offer children a range of strategies to use when difficulties arise and encourage them to be persistent learners with a 'can do' attitude as discussed in Chapter 4.

Learning needs to be connected to children's lives so that they feel central to it and have a sense of ownership over their learning. We can achieve this by ensuring that we start with the children when planning tasks and activities, use our knowledge of their interests, motivations and fascinations as a starting point and keep them central to everything we do. Whenever possible, we must allow children to experience things for themselves and have hands on experiences to deepen their knowledge and understanding about the world and how it works.

We must plan an effective learning environment with open-ended, challenging and stimulating resources. We can include new or unusual resources to keep children's interest and provide *provocations* or invitations to learn which entice children in and captivate their attention. This idea has arisen from the preschools in Reggio Emilia, Northern Italy, where they follow a child-centred approach and present resources to children in a provocative way, perhaps setting up a scene or arranging the environment in a specific way that encourages engagement and exploration. I have come across a lovely definition in a Canadian curriculum document aimed at early years practitioners:[9] 'An invitation to learn is a display of materials, carefully selected and arranged, that draws children's attention and engages them in a world of wonder, exploration, and discovery.'

ASSESSMENT OPPORTUNITIES

When assessing children's learning consider:

Being involved and concentrating

- Do the children keep focused on a self-initiated activity for a long period of time?

- Are they concentrating and involved in the activity without being distracted?

- Do they show care with what they're doing?

- Do they demonstrate concentration through silence or thinking aloud?

- Do they pay close attention to detail?

Keeping on trying

- Do children show persistence – not giving up even if it means starting again?

- Do they ask for help/support if they need it?

- Do they discuss solutions for challenges with peers/adults or work things through themselves?

- Do they bounce back after difficulties?

Enjoying achieving what they set out to do

- Is there a sense of satisfaction and pride when they have completed an activity; do they want to show/tell people?

- Do they relish challenges and continually try to make things better?

- Do they evaluate themselves and try different things as a result?

- Are they 'intrinsically motivated' – achieving things for themselves as opposed to seeking adult praise?

(Adapted from Jan Dubiel[10])

If we are successful in engaging children and motivating them to learn they will naturally maintain focus and attention, develop perseverance in learning and enjoy achieving what they set out to do. This is active learning in practice and is a great foundation for children who are transitioning to school.

REFLECTIVE PRACTICE QUESTIONS

1. To what extent do you offer children opportunities to maintain attention and focus on a variety of different activities that interest them?

2. What motivates your children and how can you use this information to plan future learning opportunities?

3. How do you ensure that children have time and freedom to become deeply involved in activities?

Notes

1. Call, N. and Featherstone, S. (2003) *The Thinking Child Resource Book.* Stafford: Network Educational Press, p.47.
2. Early Education (2012) *Development Matters in the Early Years Foundation Stage.* London: Early Education.
3. Hanscom, A. (2014) *Why children fidget.* Blog post retrieved from www.balancedandbarefoot.com/blog/the-real-reason-why-children-fidget?utm_content=buffere0b33&utm_medium=social&utm_source=twitter.com&utm_campaign=buffer, on 9 October 2017.
4. Department of Health (2011) Physical activity guidelines for early years (under 5s) for children who are capable of walking. Retrieved from https://www.gov.uk/government/uploads/system/uploads/attachment_data/file/213738/dh_128143.pdf, on 9 October 2017.

5. Hart, A., Blincow, D. and Thomas, H. (2007) *Resilient Therapy: Working with Children and Families*. London: Routledge.
6. Laevers, F. (2005) *Sics (Ziko) Manual Well-being and Involvement in Care: A process-oriented Self-evaluation Instrument for Care Settings*. Leuven, Belgium: Kind & Gezin and Research Centre for Experientel Education. Retrieved from https://www.kindengezin.be/img/sics-ziko-manual.pdf, on 9 October 2017.
7. Fisher, J. (2016) *Interacting or Interfering? Improving Interactions in the Early Years*. Maidenhead: Open University Press.
8. Vygotsky, L. (1978) *Mind in Society: The Development of Higher Psychological Processes*. Boston, MA: Harvard University.
9. Saskatchewan Online Curriculum (2010) Creating Invitations for Learning Supporting Kindergarten. Retrieved from https://www.edonline.sk.ca/bbcswebdav/library/Curriculum%20Website/Kindergarten/Resources/Core/creating_invitations_for_learning.pdf, on 9 October 2017.
10. Dubiel, J. (2012) Learning and Development: How Children Learn: Part 1 - In the process. *Nursery World*, 2 March, 2012.

6

Creating and Thinking Critically

CHAPTER OBJECTIVE

This chapter will unpick the characteristic of creating and thinking critically and relate it to children. It will consider practical ways of supporting creating and thinking critically and also consider the notion of *Sustained Shared Thinking* and how this links in with helping children to be school ready.

It is very difficult to stop thinking; we think about what to wear, where to go, when to do things, how we should do them and why things happen the way they do. Therefore thinking skills are important skills to foster. A phrase, famously attributed to Socrates, states, 'I cannot teach anybody anything, I can only make them think.' This describes our role as adults supporting children with this characteristic. Creating and thinking critically is about children who have ideas, problem solve, notice links and patterns, and can predict, review and plan how to undertake a task.

Thinking is a generic term used to describe the process of reasoning and considering something – that is, using our intellect. There are different ways that we can think. For example, if I was in the supermarket and was thinking about which punnets of strawberries to buy, I would be calculating prices, thinking ahead, comparing 'use by' dates with when I realistically thought we would finish eating the strawberries and so on. However, if I were in the garden deciding what seeds to plant and where, I would be speculating which flowerbed received most sunshine, planning the design of the garden and imagining how it would look once the flowers had grown. Both scenarios require me to think, but both involve very different skills and different types of thinking. We need to reflect on these types of thinking to ensure that we encourage children to use a variety.

MARION DOWLING'S TYPES OF THINKING[1]

We may see children:

- Planning, predicting, thinking ahead, speculating

- Investigating, exploring, gathering and using information

- Solving problems, working things out, finding solutions

- Reasoning, using their logic, explaining, making connections

- Creating, innovating, imagining new situations, fantasising

- Reflecting, recalling, sorting out feelings.

Children have more limited experiences of the world than adults, therefore their thinking differs to ours. Sometimes what they say may seem bizarre or strange or may be a total fabrication; however there will always be some sort of connection. This is because they take what knowledge (sometimes limited) they have of a particular thing, apply it to the situation, extend it with new discoveries and make their own deductions.

We can work out what children are thinking by observing them closely and noticing their facial expressions, body language and gestures in addition to listening to what they say. We need to notice what they talk about while they play and what questions they ask. Children's thinking also becomes visible through their self-chosen activities and through the way they approach a task or activity.

In the guidance document *Development Matters*,[2] creating and thinking critically is divided into three sub-headings: having their own ideas, making links and choosing ways to do things. This chapter considers case studies about children and relates them to each of these aspects. It is difficult to look at one characteristic in isolation as these children are also playing and exploring and demonstrating that they are active learners; however for the purposes of this chapter I have only related them to creating and thinking critically.

Irena (3 years 4 months) was in the nursery garden helping a practitioner water the flowers in the border with a watering can when she crouched down, picked up a stick and started to stir the mud. She then poured more water on the ground and stirred again. She said, 'There's a hole in the puddle' then poured more water and watched closely. She repeated this until she ran out of water.

While Robert and Andrew were sitting on the carpet in their Reception class, Robert leaned over and banged his head on the floor! He then turned to Andrew and said, 'See!' The teacher asked Robert what he was doing and he said, 'I'm just showing Andrew that you don't really get stars around your head...'

Amina (3 years 7 months) had been finding out about shapes. She came into the preschool room and pointed at the window and said, 'Look, a rectangle!' Later, during snack time Amina noticed the hole in the back of the plastic chair, 'Look, an oval!'

When the playgroup leader told the children that they were going on a walk to a forest, Zena (nearly 3 years old) said, 'We might see elephants there!'

During a *forest school* session, Isaac was investigating the logs and pieces of wood, some of  which had ridges cut in them, and had been collated for children to explore. He began by using both hands to lift a log, but dropped it, perhaps because it was too heavy, so Isaac picked up a smaller stick and started tapping the logs with it. He also found that if he scraped the logs with his stick it made an interesting sound. Isaac also investigated the holes in the wood and began slotting the smaller sticks into the holes in the larger logs.

In the large hall after he had been exercising rigorously, Mohammed (4 years 8 months) put both hands on his chest, panted and said, 'My heart is breaking!'

Having their own ideas

As practitioners we must observe and actively listen, then try to figure out what the children are thinking. Irena is being creative as she actively explores the mud, and when she notices that the water disappears, she uses her knowledge of holes to deduce that there must be a hole in the puddle! Irena is investigating, exploring, using her logic and speculating, which are all different types of thinking.

Robert has thought of a way of demonstrating to Andrew his point of view, that after a bump to the head, one doesn't actually get stars around it! He is proving his point literally. Perhaps these boys have watched some cartoons when they see a character depicted as dizzy by the illustrator drawing stars around their head. Young children find it difficult to differentiate reality from fantasy and this anecdote captures this confusion.

Zena is also applying logic as she predicts the animals they might see during their trip to the forest. Perhaps Zena has recently read some books about Elmer,[3] the patchwork elephant who is often illustrated in a forest. She may not have had any first hand experiences of visiting a forest or wood and is using her knowledge from stories that she has listened to, and perhaps non-fiction books about elephants living in forests.

Isaac is developing his own ideas when he thinks about different ways that he can use the resources during the forest school session. He has time to explore the logs and sticks and investigate how he can interact with them.

Mohammed is noticing the changes in his body as he exercises. His heart rate has increased and he may not have been aware of this feeling before.

Another element relating to creating and thinking critically is problem solving. This is an important skill that will help children to deal with many issues they may encounter throughout life. There are several opportunities for children to solve problems throughout the day, as we saw in Chapter 5, when Bailey wanted to find a way of attaching the card apex to his rocket design. Isaac, to a lesser extent, was problem solving when he was trying to work out how to play with the logs and sticks during the forest school session. In addition, if two children want to use the same toy and conflicts arise we can use the problem solving approach from *HighScope*,[4] discussed in Chapter 9, to turn the situation into a learning opportunity.

Making links

This element of creating and thinking critically is about children who are able to make links and notice patterns in their experience, like Amina, who is noticing similarities between the shapes she has learned about and the shapes in the environment around her. We do this too; our brains are constantly looking for meaning and affirmation. For example, you may have noticed that if you have ever purchased a new car, you will have carefully researched which car to buy and then when you drive it home, suddenly the same car is everywhere! You had hardly noticed them before but now it feels as if everyone is driving the same model! Your brain is making links.

Irena is testing her ideas about holes and making links with her understanding about water disappearing though holes, perhaps from observing the bath water going down the plughole. She is also investigating cause and effect as she pours the water and it sinks in to the ground.

Robert is reasoning and explaining his to his friend what he thinks. He is testing his idea that you don't get stars around your head after a bump and attempting to prove this to Andrew. Zena is also sharing her knowledge with another person as she tells the playgroup leader her prediction about what she might see in the forest. She is thinking ahead, speculating and making an educated guess relating to the animals that could live there.

We can try to work out what Mohammed is thinking by analysing the language he uses. He might have heard a phrase relating to a heart breaking and he is putting two and two together and assuming that this is what he is feeling. Of course, Mohammed might have muddled up his words and meant to say, 'My heart is beating', but used the word 'breaking' by mistake. Children are learning new words, often on a daily basis, and do not always use new words in context. If Mohammed deliberately said 'breaking' we might want to reassure him that his heart is not broken in any way and actually what he is feeling is perfectly normal and healthy.

TOP 5 WAYS TO PROMOTE CHILDREN'S THINKING SKILLS

1. Use the language of thinking and learning, for example, think, wonder, decide, imagine, agree, disagree, find out, make sense, plan, have an idea, problem solve, figure out, know, try to.

2. Role model being a thinker. Talk aloud as you do things, explaining to yourself your reasoning, for example, I think I'm going to put this block here. It's the right shape to be a roof for my house.

3. Engage in Sustained Shared Thinking, getting involved in the thinking process with the children.

4. Give feedback to children, label-praise and help children to review their own progress and learning.

5. Provide opportunities for children to problem solve and turn any problems that arise throughout the day into learning opportunities.

Choosing ways to do things

In Chapter 3 we came across Marie who was making a sandwich. She planned the task, discussing with her parent the ingredients that she needed and decided for herself how to approach the task. In a similar way, Irena was deciding what to do as she explored the water sinking into the ground.

Isaac was thinking about how to use the resources and began by trying to lift the log. It was quite heavy and he dropped it, which led him to change strategy and think of a different way to use the resources. He then tapped the logs using the smaller stick as a beater and changed his approach again by scraping the stick over the logs. Isaac was investigating the different noises that he could make by tapping and scraping first hand. Later on he developed his ideas further by inserting sticks into the holes in the logs.

Bailey, who we met in Chapter 5, was planning how to make his rocket. He frequently checked how well he was doing and changed strategy when he was unable to attach the apex of the rocket onto his design. This involved a lot of thinking and required him to be flexible in his approach. He learned that there are many possible ways of attaching things together, and some will be better suited to certain tasks than others.

Very young children are mostly working at Piaget's[5] *pre-operational* or *concrete operational stage of cognitive development* so find abstract thinking difficult. We need to model this with children, reflecting on their progress and suggesting ideas for improvement. We can encourage children to reflect upon their learning by talking to them about their decisions and discuss alternative ways forward. We can model the process of reviewing, by talking about what worked well and what we would like to change next time. Many settings operate a *plan-do-review* approach, which can help children to develop thinking skills.

Creating and thinking critically – an element of school readiness

The stories about children shared in this and other chapters demonstrate creating and thinking critically, which is, in my view giving them a foundation on which to learn at school. If we consider the school environment we can imagine many scenarios when children are expected to think for themselves, problem solve and review their work. Many classes invite children to think about their own next steps, reflecting on their learning and thinking about what they might improve in the future.

I can talk about my learning

I do not understand yet. I need help.

I am beginning to understand this and only need a little help.

I understand and can explain it to my friend.

Most schools talk to children in terms of learning, for example using acronyms such as WALT (We Are Learning To) and WILF (What I'm Looking For) or introduce lessons by sharing *success criteria* or *learning objectives*: what teachers expect children to achieve during the lesson. This can sound a little over the top; however, it is really helpful for children. Imagine that you were writing a report at work and you were not given any guidance as to what you should include in the report. You would probably feel very vulnerable and would want more guidance. In a similar way, it can be helpful if children know what they are learning about. It is vital, however, that our youngest children are not pushed into a formal learning situation at too young an age, therefore talk things through using simple language and phrases which introduce the language of thinking and learning in developmentally appropriate ways.

Within school there will be opportunities for children to have their own ideas and voice their opinions as well as times when children can share their news from home. Children will make connections between school, home and the communities they live in, noticing similarities and differences between themselves and their friends' lives. By providing children with the opportunity to foster the characteristic of creating and thinking critically, we are enabling children to become 'thinkers' and helping to prepare them for school.

The role of the adult in supporting creating and thinking critically

There are many ways in which to support children in creating and thinking critically. We need to offer children thinking time so that they can think things through without having to dive straight in. We can also role model the thinking process ourselves, sometimes thinking aloud whilst we play alongside the children. We can interact with children sensitively, offering interesting, exciting and stimulating resources and activities and engaging in Sustained Shared Thinking.

Sustained Shared Thinking (SST) is a term that arose from the EPPE research project[6] in the UK. It relates to adults engaging in the thinking process with children, for example, working together to develop an idea or skill, asking open-ended questions, clarifying concepts and problem solving. Although a fairly new term, it describes an older concept. It links in with the idea of adults *scaffolding* learning and supporting children to develop and extend their thinking. The EPPE research considered quality practice and identified more SST in settings where children made the most progress. This type of thinking can only happen when there are responsive trusting relationships between adults and children and where the adult shows genuine interest and offers encouragement to the children.

The EPPE research also found that in the most effective settings, practitioners used open-ended questioning to support children's thinking. It is important not to bombard children with questions, but ask a few appropriate questions that will prompt further investigation. We can also value and encourage children to ask questions themselves to find things out. Why? What? When? Where? Who? We must try not to rush into answering all their questions immediately, rather, serve the ball back to them by asking what they think.

One setting presented interesting ideas to the children and discussed 'what if' scenarios. Once they had a long discussion about 'what if the sea was red and the sky was yellow?' which led to the children investigating colour mixing and sunsets. They found that the more unusual and silly the suggestion, the more the children wanted to engage with it and talk about it!

A really useful observational tool has been created which assesses practice in relation to Sustained Shared Thinking. The Sustained Shared Thinking and Emotional Wellbeing Scale[7] (SSTEW) can be used for research or self-evaluation and improvement and will assist practitioners in evaluating their practice. One of the areas considered within the scale is 'supporting learning and critical thinking'.

SUPPORTING SUSTAINED SHARED THINKING

Iram Siraj-Blatchford[8] identifies the following range of strategies to support Sustained Shared Thinking:

- **Tuning in:** listening carefully to what is being said, observing body language and what the child is doing.

- **Showing interest:** giving their whole attention to the child, maintaining eye contact, smiling, nodding.

- **Respecting children's own decisions and choices by inviting children to elaborate:** saying things like 'I really want to know more about this' and listening and engaging in the response.

- **Re-capping:** 'So you think that...'

- **Offering the adult's own experience:** 'I like to listen to music when I cook supper at home.'

- **Clarifying ideas:** 'Right, Darren, so you think that this stone will melt if I boil it in water?'

- **Suggesting:** 'You might like to try doing it this way.'

- **Reminding:** 'Don't forget that you said this stone will melt if I boil it.'

- **Using encouragement to further thinking:** 'You have really thought hard about where to put this door in the palace – where will you put the windows?'

- **Offering an alternative viewpoint:** 'Maybe Goldilocks wasn't naughty when she ate the porridge?'

- **Speculating:** 'Do you think the three bears would have liked Goldilocks to come to live with them as their friend?'

- **Reciprocating:** 'Thank goodness you were wearing wellie boots when you jumped in those puddles. Look at my feet, they're soaking wet!'

- **Asking open questions:** 'How did you...?' 'Why does this...?' 'What happens next?' 'What do you think?' 'I wonder what would happen if...?'

- **Modelling thinking:** 'I have to think hard about what I do this evening. I need to take my dog to the vet because he has a sore foot, take my library books back to the library and buy some food for dinner tonight. But I just won't have time to do all of these things.'

If we consider the case studies in this chapter, a skilful practitioner will pick up on Irena's interest and offer her further opportunities to explore the concept of the water sinking into the ground. Perhaps asking her some 'What will happen if...?' questions to prompt her to think more deeply about what she is noticing. Robert and Andrew may also want to think about what happens when we bang our heads and share their ideas with others.

We can support Amina in creating and thinking critically, by encouraging her to make more links between the shapes she is learning about and the shapes in the environment. She might enjoy going on a shape hunt in the outside area and looking for other shapes that are naturally found.

We can support and extend Zena's thinking by talking with her about animals that live in our country. We should value her ideas, saying something like, 'So you think that we might see elephants in the forest? That's an interesting idea. How can we find out which animals might live in forests in our country?' With adult help, Zena might be interested in researching this further using books or the

Internet. Alternatively, we might choose to reflect on this conversation after the visit to the forest and ask Zena if we did see any elephants and if not, why not?

We can also support children's thinking by providing a learning environment with open-ended, flexible resources and an ethos that promotes thinking. This will encourage children to be independent and autonomous in their learning, like Isaac, who was confident to explore the various resources he found during the forest school session. He was free to experiment and try out his ideas, without being confined by thinking that there was a 'right' way to use the logs and sticks.

When children's thinking becomes visible through the language they use, we can explore the concepts further with them. For example, we can talk with Mohammed about how he feels and get him to think about any other changes he has noticed in his body from exercising. We could also encourage him to investigate his heart beat and breathing at different times throughout the day.

ASSESSMENT OPPORTUNITIES

When assessing children's learning consider:

Having their own ideas

- Do they try something different rather than follow what someone else has done?
- Do they address a problem with a strategy?
- Can they think of new ways to do things?

Making links

- Do they notice and understand patterns and predictability of events?
- Do they talk about/explain how their process links to a previous experience?

- Can they test their ideas and think about cause and effect?

- Do they draw upon knowledge or experiences not immediately related to their activity?

Choosing ways to do things

- Can they plan, make decisions about how to approach a task/solve a problem?

- Are they confident in using a 'trial and error' approach and talking about why some things do/don't work?

- Do they review their work or check how well their activities are going?

- Can they choose different ways of approaching activities and adapt them if they don't work?

- Can they review strategies they use?

(Adapted from Jan Dubiel[9])

When we listen to and value children's ideas, support them to problem solve, encourage them to make links and notice patterns in their learning we are supporting children to become thinkers. Offering children choices and allowing them to make decisions will empower them to think critically and they will thrive in school in an environment where thinking is vital. Loris Malaguzi,[10] the initial teacher and founder of the preschools in Reggio Emelia, sums up our role as practitioners with regard to creating and thinking critically beautifully, saying, 'Our task, regarding creativity, is to help children climb their own mountains, as high as possible. No one can do more.'

REFLECTIVE PRACTICE QUESTIONS

1. How do you involve children in thinking about their learning?

2. What opportunities are there for you to engage in Sustained Shared Thinking with children during a typical session?

3. In what ways do you help children to climb their own mountains?

Notes

1. Dowling, M. (2005) *Supporting Young Children's Sustained Shared Thinking: An Exploration.* London: British Association for Early Childhood Education, p.8.
2. Early Education (2012) *Development Matters in the Early Years Foundation Stage.* London: Early Education.
3. Mckee, D. (2007) *Elmer.* London: Andersen Press.
4. HighScope Educational Research Foundation (2017) How does High/scope help children learn how to resolve conflicts? Retrieved from https://highscope.org/faq, on 9 October 2017.
5. Piaget, J. and Inhelder, B. (2000) *The Psychology of the Child*, 2nd edn. New York: Basic Books.
6. Siraj-Blatchford, I. and Taggart, B. (eds) (2010) *Early Childhood Matters: Evidence from the Effective Pre-school and Primary Education Project.* Abingdon: Routledge.
7. Siraj, I., Kingston, D. and Melhuish, E. (2015) *Assessing Quality in Early Childhood Education and Care: Sustained Shared Thinking and Emotional Well-being (SSTEW) Scale for 2–5-year-olds Provision.* London: IOE Press.
8. Siraj-Blatchford, I. (2005) 'Quality interactions in the early years.' Paper presented at TACTYC Annual Conference in Cardiff on 5 November 2005. Retrieved from www.tactyc.org.uk/pdfs/2005conf_siraj.pdf, on 9 October 2017, pp.9–12.
9. Dubiel, J. (2012) Learning and Development: How Children Learn: Part 1 – In the process. *Nursery World*, 2 April, 2012.
10. Edwards, C., Gandini, L. and Forman, G. (eds) (1998) *The Hundred Languages of Children: The Reggio Emilia Approach –Advanced Reflections*, 2nd edn. London: JAI Press Ltd, p.77.

7

Children Who Are Ready

CHAPTER OBJECTIVE

This chapter will focus on readiness in terms of the children. It will consider children's own views on transition and how schools and settings can better support children through this phase.

When considering school readiness and children beginning school, children should be central to the discussion. It felt appropriate for me to dedicate a chapter of this book to children, although it is my intention that children's centrality is implicit throughout every chapter. Often authors and theorists refer to the voice of the child. This can be a helpful way of ensuring that children's views are captured, however it is important to remember that we can choose not to listen to a voice. We can turn the volume down on the voice, or even switch it off, if it makes us feel uncomfortable! Perhaps a better analogy is to think about children's presence. If children are present in the debate about school readiness, it will be harder to ignore them.

We need to ensure that we listen to children to gather their views and opinions. True listening is not a passive process; it demands something from us and provokes an emotional, physical and intellectual response. One listening method that is used is 'consultation'. This term has occasionally been used interchangeably with other terms such as 'listening' and 'participation' in order to tick the 'voice of the child' box. However, as Malcolm Hill[1] and his colleagues from various Scottish universities point out, consultation is often driven by policy-makers who have their own agenda. Consultation tends to generalise about children's views and we need to zoom in on the families and children at the heart of the issue. This is effective practice in the early years, starting with the child and looking at their individual needs.

This chapter shares some thoughts relating to children who are ready and perhaps those who are not ready for school. I touch on ideas such as developmental readiness and how to ascertain the views of children, as well as considering some general ideas about how to support children through transitions. I give the last word to the children who share some thoughts about starting school.

Developmental readiness

The EYFS[2] states that 'Children develop and learn in different ways and at different rates.' When you think about a typical four–year-old, one year in their life at this age is a quarter of their whole life! Put in these terms, it is no wonder that they are all different. Let's think about developmental milestones for a moment. Some children are fast walkers but slow to talk, others crawl at a very young age but seem to take forever to walk! The same is true throughout childhood and it is impossible to say that all children will talk by one year old or all children will walk by 16 months. Child development does not appear to be a linear process with one blueprint that fits all children.

When we consider children starting school and how ready they are for this phase of education in the light of this, it is vital that we bear in mind these individual differences and do not have a one-size-fits-all approach. We need to think about children being developmentally ready for school and this will be at different times for different children.

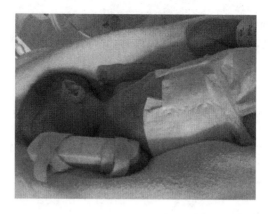

Simon was born prematurely at 33 weeks and weighed just 3lb 6oz (1.5kg). He was due on the 12 October and arrived bright and early on the 27 August. I first met Simon when he was two months old and he was still really tiny. He remains smaller than average for his age, but fortunately has not suffered any developmental delay or complications due to being premature. He is now a lively five–year–old.

In terms of premature babies, midwives and health visitors take into account the fact that a baby is premature when looking at their development milestones. When it comes to school intakes, this point is often overlooked. When we consider starting school, Simon was born into the year group above the one he would have been in if he were born full term. He began in a Reception class just one week after his fourth birthday. Was Simon school ready? No! He tried his hardest at school but he found sitting and concentrating even for small amounts of time really hard. He needed to be active, to focus on the Prime Areas of Physical Development, Communication and Language and Personal, Social and Emotional Development rather than slot into daily phonics sessions with his peers.

Simon's mother was really happy with the school's focus on play and active learning, however, when asked if she felt he was ready for school, she immediately replied, 'No!' Given half the chance she would have kept him off for another year or longer, but feared that in doing so he would find it harder to make friends entering his year group in Year 1 when the other children would have had a whole year together in Reception.

In recent years in the UK, admissions arrangements have become a little more flexible when they relate to summer born children and other children with exceptional circumstances like Simon. Bliss,[3] the charity for babies born prematurely or sick, offers advice and guidance on starting school in England for parents like Simon's who may want to defer their child's entry to school.

However there are many other children who would benefit from a later start to school as Chapter 2 has discussed. If schools were able to focus on developmental readiness Simon would not have been expected to conform to a system that doesn't meet his needs.

Early intervention

The Equality Act (2010)[4] requires schools and settings to make **reasonable adjustments** for children with SEND. In my experience, teachers in schools tend to have such a huge workload, keeping up with all the red-tape and paperwork that the role demands, that they probably can't quote you chapter and verse of the Equality Act. This is understandable, but it is important that schools also consider what reasonable adjustments would look like for the children in their care.

> David will be 4 years and 8 months when he starts in the local Reception class. He is not yet toilet trained and the school has explained to his parents that they do not have the facilities to change nappies or clothing so regrettably have arranged for his parents to come into school every time he has an accident or needs his 'pull-up' changed. David's nursery setting is concerned that he may have additional needs and have flagged this up with school. They have asked his parents to take him to his Health Visitor to discuss his development.

The vast majority of children are continent when they go to Primary school and are no longer wearing nappies or pull-ups. To comply with the Equality Act, it is not acceptable for a school to refuse admission to a child who is not yet toilet trained; however, many schools like David's are placing unreasonable requests on parents relating to their child's continence. According to ERIC,[5] the children's bowel and bladder charity, 'A delay in achieving continence – or not being toilet trained – can be considered a disability' and when talking about children who are still incontinent, schools 'must work to support those children in the school environment so they can play an active role in school life, remain healthy and achieve their academic potential'.

David's Primary school is not ready for David. They need to think about ways to support him and getting around the toileting issue is one of them. His school needs to think about what they can do in terms of reasonable adjustments to support David in his learning and development. ERIC[6] uses very strong terms when it talks about parents being asked to come in and change a child, 'It is tantamount to abuse to force a child to sit in wet or soiled underwear until their parent or guardian can come in to change them.' Therefore, the 'solution' that the school have come up with is not acceptable for David. On a practical note, sometimes the request for a parent to come and change the child arises from an assumption that two adults will be needed to change the child, however this is not the case and intimate care routines only need more than one adult if a child's care plan specifies this.[7]

Almost all respondents to my survey, mentioned in Chapter 1, felt that school readiness related to self-care, including toileting. Does this mean that David is not ready for school? Is it fair to assume this? David is still developing his ability to manage his own hygiene needs, however going to the toilet takes up a very small amount of a very long school day. His nursery has flagged up that he may have additional needs, but we are unsure exactly what these are. We do know that he will have interests and fascinations of his own and he may well be ready for school in other areas. His school needs to get to know David, work out what he likes to do and plan an exciting and interesting learning environment within which he can play, explore and learn. A great way in would be to consider the Characteristics of Effective Learning (CoEL) in relation to David's skills and abilities.

Early intervention is vital when it comes to addressing children's needs. The sooner children can be identified as needing additional support, the earlier support can put in place to help them. I have had many discussions with parents and practitioners who believe that this is labelling children and an unhelpful way forward, however, my view is that the name or label is not important, but meeting a child's needs is vital and sometimes the only way to ensure that a child's needs are fully met is to go down the formal diagnosis route. Early identification requires schools and settings to work in partnership with parents and collaborate together over the needs of the child. Chapters 9 and 10 look into this further.

Supporting children through change and transitions

When I talk to practitioners about change, I often ask them to put their watch on the other wrist, or swap a ring to the other hand. Although only a tiny change, it can feel really odd and uncomfortable. We need to support children through any processes involving change and starting school for the first time is a huge milestone for them. This change can be planned for and carefully implemented over time, ensuring that the children are involved in every stage as it should come as no surprise that school is looming. Other changes might be spontaneous or sudden and cannot be planned for in advance; however we can still ensure that children are involved at every stage.

Adults can sometimes view changes, like starting school, as exciting; however for many children school is unknown, unpredictable and even scary. We might notice a deterioration in our child's behaviour as they anticipate starting school, or they may simply become unsettled. Although it is important to prepare children for starting school as much as possible, we must avoid talking about it too much. We can build things up into a mountain and over-hype this phase, when some children may have needed us to be calmer and more matter of fact about the transition.

IDEAS FOR SUPPORTING CHILDREN THROUGH CHANGE

- Discuss the issue with the children and provide them with the rationale behind the change.

- Seek to find out children's views about the changes.

- Allow the children to own as many of the changes as possible and value their contribution to the process.

- Break the change down into smaller steps or stages and if possible implement over time.

- Prepare for the change as much as possible, for example visit the new school, engage in their transition arrangements, try on the uniform, undertake a practice journey to school, and so on.

- Avoid over-stressing about the change and building it up too much.

- Keep to your usual routines to provide consistency and security to the children.

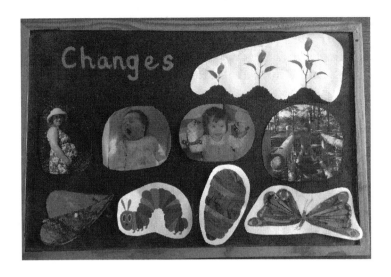

Readiness for a child

To be ready is about being fully prepared for something or in a position to act immediately. However, in asking if children are ready for school are we attaching adult concepts and language to the children? Do children understand all the intricacies of being ready for school and is it appropriate to expect this? If a child says, 'I'm ready' what does this mean? Have they thought through all of the possible scenarios they might find themselves presented with and prepared in advance? Perhaps an alternative and more appropriate definition of readiness could also include being willing or eager, thus readiness for a child could be about instilling in them a sense of excitement and eagerness for school.

Looking at readiness in terms of a willingness to learn helps to remove the tick box definitions of being prepared. We can then look to the dispositions and attitudes needed for a child to be ready to learn. This links closely with Carol Dweck's idea of mindsets.[8] She suggests that most people fit into two categories: those with a *fixed mindset* and those with a *growth mindset*. Children who develop a fixed mindset will limit themselves and be more likely to give up in the face of adversity whereas those with a growth mindset are more resilient and able to learn through any mistakes. The possibilities are endless for these children. Dweck also found that younger children are not as concerned with making mistakes per se but rather with 'goodness' and 'badness'. If an adult were to pick up on the mistake and criticise it in some way, the child showed more signs of helplessness and having a fixed mindset. Therefore, our adult response to children is critical and will help to determine the beliefs that children develop regarding their goals and reactions to any setbacks.

TOP 5 WAYS TO FOSTER A GROWTH MINDSET

1. Offer encouragement and praise the process children are involved in, not the intelligence or outcome, for example, 'You put a lot of thought into that!'

2. Value all setbacks and mistakes as opportunities to discover and learn.

3. Be slow to provide answers and quick to problem solve. Teach and model strategies like problem solving techniques so that if children get stuck they can try to figure it out.

4. Foster the CoEL – encourage a 'can do' attitude, perseverance, resilience and thinking skills.

5. Help children to reframe their thinking about themselves, for instance rephrase, 'I'm not good at doing up buttons' to 'I am learning to do up buttons', or rephrase, 'I can't do it' to 'Let's try and find another way of doing it!'

What do children think?

According to article 12 in the UN Convention on the Rights of the Child,[9] children have the right to express their views freely, if they are deemed capable of having views and according to their age and stage of maturity and development. However there is little research into the views of primary age children and younger with regard to starting school.

One study attempted to find out children's opinions in terms of starting school and how ready they felt. In the year 2000, 54 children were interviewed in Victoria, Australia, when they started school and again three years later and the results were recorded.[10] They found that children identified difficulties such as understanding the language the teachers used and feeling that there was less time for play. Knowing and conforming to school rules also arose as an issue. The study went on to suggest that there are many ways that schools and settings can help children within these areas, for example by teaching children the classroom rules and procedures before they start as well as supporting peer relationships and social skills.

In order to ascertain what children think we need to listen to them. As previously mentioned, listening to young children is a recurring theme within the early years sector with many settings adopting the *mosaic approach*,[11] which considers the views of young children and attempts to respond and actively listen to their perspective. Thus considering children's views in a holistic way will help to keep the child at the heart of early years practice.

KEEPING CHILDREN PRESENT AND FINDING OUT THEIR VIEWS

You can find out the views of young children by:

- observing where they play
- observing what they play with/their interests

- listening to them while they play or talk with their peers

- observing their body language and gestures

- giving the children cameras to take photos of the areas or resources they like best in your setting

- encouraging the children to draw their favourite thing

- asking them to cut pictures out of a resource catalogue relating to things that they like or are interested in

- giving children pictures to sort into like/dislike

- mapping areas with the children and drawing plans of the setting

- engaging in child conferencing – asking children simple questions to ascertain their views

- asking the children to take you on a tour of their setting/play spaces

- role playing with the children and listening to what they say during imaginative play

- holding a group discussion and encouraging the children to share their thoughts and ideas

- asking parents for the views of their child – remember that this will be their perception of their child's views.

As part of my research for this book I tried to ascertain the views of some children. I was very aware of the ethical issues surrounding gathering the views of children. If I knew the children well, I engaged in conversation with them on an informal basis; if I didn't have a secure relationship with them I asked parents to casually chat to their children.

I offered parents some questions to help guide their discussions.

'I was glad my preschool friend was going to the same school as me, but I made new friends as well.'

Pippa on starting school

Here are some top tips that the children gave me to share with other children who are about to start school. I have recorded their answers verbatim to prevent me from rephrasing and perhaps misinterpreting their meaning.

- Know your way around.
- Know the dinner bell.
- Make friends.
- If you feel sad call a teacher.
- Teachers are here to help you.
- Try your best.
- Have fun.
- Try to be a good learner.
- Play happily.
- Just be calm.
- Remember to listen to the teacher very well.
- Write really neatly.
- If you don't know much don't worry you can ask people.
- Listen to the teacher.
- Be kind and say well done to your friends.
- Be happy.
- Know what to do in the classroom.

We can learn from these children and try to incorporate their ideas into our practice by sharing these messages with the children in our care who are about to start school. They provide us with an insight into what they value and sometimes a reflection on what they wish they knew beforehand. In a similar way, their responses to my question about overcoming their worries provides us with a privileged glimpse into their thoughts. We can use this to help to curb the potential worries that other children might have. For example, friendship arises as a way of feeling less worried, therefore we must do everything in our power to ensure that children begin school knowing a few other children, and feel like they have friends.

When I asked what made children feel better when they were worried about school, they provided the following responses:

- Teachers were nice.

- My best friend was there.

- Having a packed lunch.

- Making friends.

- That I made lots of friends.

- Someone to cuddle me, sitting and reading.

- When I saw my friends there that I already knew.

- Playing with my friends.

- Lots of cuddles from my family.

One little girl who is about to start school in September told me that she was looking forward to school because she wanted, 'to read books, because I want to read myself a story'. She has associated reading with school. She also said she wanted, 'to meet my old friends from preschool' and 'to get a star'. Her older brother had already informed her about their star reward system and it has had a big impact on her. She also liked the fact that the teachers wear necklaces, which I am guessing are name tag lanyards! After her school visit, when her mother asked why she liked her teachers she said, 'because they play with me' and 'they help me with my PE things'.

These are very insightful comments from a child so young. She has picked up on the social, cognitive and behavioural aspects of school, mostly learned from her older sibling. She is ready, willing and able to learn and I'm sure will thrive in school.

I also asked my own children about their views on starting school and school in general. This led to an amusing conversation about school dinners with my daughter who was five years old and in a Reception class. She wanted to improve the school dinners and planned and designed her own school dinner. We then made the dinner at home as a trial. It was beans on toast. As you can see, there was a thorough plan and I was left in no doubt about how to present the meal!

REFLECTIVE PRACTICE QUESTIONS

1. What does school readiness mean from the perspective of the child? How do you know?

2. What do policy-makers/teachers/parents/practitioners think a child's needs are? Is there a gap between this and their actual needs?

3. How do you ensure the presence of children in your decision making processes?

Notes

1. Hill, M., Davis, J., Prout, A. and Tisdall, K. (2004) 'Moving the participation agenda forward.' *Children and Society,* 18(2), 77–96.
2. Department for Education (DfE) (2017) *Statutory Framework for the Early Years Foundation Stage.* Retrieved from www.foundationyears.org.uk/files/2017/03/EYFS_STATUTORY_FRAMEWORK_2017.pdf, on 9 October 2017, p.6.
3. Bliss for babies born premature or sick, https://www.bliss.org.uk/
4. Council for Disabled Children (2015) *Disabled Children and the Equality Act 2010.* Retrieved from https://councilfordisabledchildren.org.uk/sites/default/files/field/attachemnt/equality-act-early-years_online.pdf, 9 October 2017.
5. ERIC (2017) Retrieved from https://www.eric.org.uk/toileting-best-practice-at-school, on 9 October 2017.
6. ERIC (2017).
7. Safer Recruitment Consortium (2015) *Guidance for safer working practice for those working with children and young people in education settings.* Retrieved from https://www.safeguardinginschools.co.uk/wp-content/uploads/2015/10/Guidance-for-Safer-Working-Practices-2015-final1.pdf, on 9 October 2017, p.14.
8. Dweck, C. (2017) 'The journey to children's mindsets – and beyond.' *Child Development Perspectives,* 11(2), 139–144.
9. UNICEF (1989) United Nations Convention on the Rights of the Child. Retrieved from www.unicef.org.uk/Documents/Publication-pdfs/UNCRC_PRESS 200910web.pdf, on 9 October 2017.
10. Margetts, K. (2013) 'What New Children Need to Know: Children's Perspectives of Starting School.' In K. Margetts and A. Kienig (eds) *International Perspectives on Transition to School: Reconceptualising Beliefs, Policy and Practice.* Abingdon: Routledge.
11. Clark, A. and Moss, P. (2011) *Listening to Young Children: The Mosaic Approach,* 2nd edn. London: NCB.

8

Children-ready Schools

CHAPTER OBJECTIVE

This chapter will focus on ways in which schools can ensure that they are ready for the children they receive in Reception classes. It shares some stories about how schools have engaged children and offers practical ideas and suggestions of ways to improve practice.

There is a lot of talk about preparing children for school in relation to school readiness; however I want to shift the focus onto how schools actively prepare themselves for children. At a recent event Andreas Schleicher,[1] director for education and skills at the Organisation for Economic Co-operation and Development (OECD), said, 'We need to do more on making schools ready for children, not children ready for school.' He based these comments on the findings from the recent report that summarises the OECD study, *Starting Strong 2017*,[2] which considers the latest research and thinking on early childhood education and care policies and practices in 30 OECD countries and partner countries. It raises the issue that play is diminishing and warns against schoolification as discussed in Chapter 2.

Schools have a responsibility to be ready for the children that arrive through their doors. Their work does not begin with a cohort of children in September when the children first start school, but rather it starts much earlier in the year when teachers are planning ahead and thinking about the next group due to start. This is about processes being in place to support families and transition, ongoing relationships between schools and their feeder settings and also ensuring that the environment is ready for children.

This chapter will consider these issues and share some of the ideas I gained during my research. For the purposes of this book I visited specific schools to discuss their approach to school readiness and transitions. I also engaged with hundreds of other teachers and practitioners who shared their insights with me through face-to-face discussion and notes on a paper questionnaire. I hope that this chapter represents their views as well as my own. Being children-ready is more about an approach to teaching rather than a recipe to follow and each school will want to cater for the unique needs of their children. Thus there is not a one-size-fits-all approach.

The purpose of the Reception class

In England and Wales the Reception class, or YR, is the first main class in a maintained school which children usually enter in the September following their fourth birthday. As discussed in Chapter 2, *statutory school age* is the term after a child's fifth birthday so for the majority of children this will fall during the Reception year. This year, as its name suggests, is traditionally thought of as 'receiving' the child into school. It is a gentle introduction to school routines and culture. It is also the oldest age group in the EYFS, before children progress on to Key Stage 1.

Historically the early years has been seen as a phase in its own right, almost like a Key Stage. However, unfortunately, since the introduction of the EYFS, a shift has taken place. Now, early years is viewed more as being purely about preparing children for the next phase of education and 'school readiness'. The Hundred Review[3] found that, 'There is a strong belief amongst YR Practitioners, Teachers and School Leaders that an important part of the purpose of YR should be to engender young children's love of learning.'

We must ensure that we focus on fostering this love of learning rather than narrowly preparing children for school. We can do this by focusing on the Characteristics of Effective Learning (CoEL), as discussed in previous chapters. As children progress through the school, they will need to enjoy learning or risk falling behind. As Marie, a teacher a couple of years into her career, stated:

> Observing a Year 1 class as part of my teacher training showed me that in order to thrive in school, children need to be active listeners who are ready to learn by the time they are six years old. In the school I observed, the syllabus was literacy and numeracy focused and the tempo of teaching fast. Children needed to be interested in learning, enthusiastic to contribute their ideas and able to settle to the tasks set. The amount that was packed into each day felt too much and it seems wrong that so much is expected of children at such a young age.

Thus Reception class teachers have quite a balancing act to do, to ensure that children love learning and are ready for more formal teaching, whilst holding true to what they believe is the right approach for our youngest learners, focusing on active learning and playing and exploring.

YR is also an opportunity to introduce children and families to the culture of school. One headteacher described this as 'demystifying school' for families. Schools have their own jargon and all do things in different ways. Some parents may not have been in a school environment since they left at 16 years old. It is important to build a positive relationship with parents as it may set the tone for the next twelve years! Chapter 10 looks at parental engagement in more detail.

Most importantly, YR welcomes children into the school and will have a huge impact on how children view school. We want children to enjoy school, get as much as possible out of their schooling and leave having reached their potential for learning. This is about encouraging children to see themselves as learners and for us to remove as many barriers as possible along the way. Keeping the CoEL as a focus is an excellent way of ensuring that children's learning is central to our practice. One school I visited introduced the children to 'learning friends', characters which reminded the children of the skills needed to be good learners, like 'Resilient Mumble', 'Determined Bruce' and 'Focus Frog'.

Admission into YR

Many YR classes have a staggered intake of children. Occasionally this intake occurs throughout Reception year, with new children starting each term according to their age, however the majority of YR classes now have one intake in the autumn term so that the cohort spends a whole year in YR. I have found from my research that the speed at which children are admitted differs from school to school, according to their own policies and procedures and can be staggered over a few days or even a few months.

Several schools invited the children to attend trial sessions in school prior to starting full time. They organised for children to attend for half a day for a couple of days, then stay for lunch and then attend full time. All of the children were phased into school in this way, therefore all had the chance to experience playtime and lunch time in smaller groups. Another school only allowed children to visit for one session of about an hour and a half before they were in full time. According to the teacher the children coped very well, although I'm not convinced that jumping in at the deep end is the best approach! One school offered a programme of open drop-in sessions and *stay and play* sessions called 'Come and discover' throughout the previous year for families to attend. They found that the children who had attended these were better adapted to school and settled in faster. The children knew the adults in the school, felt comfortable in the environment and had already been introduced to a few school routines.

It is vital that YR teachers and leadership teams weigh up the benefits and disadvantages of a fast versus slow intake and do what they believe will be best for the children, without bowing to any pressures to speed up the process. This needs to be carefully thought through. For example, think about summer born children. They are very young and could be deemed unready for school, however, most staggered intakes receive these children last, therefore they join large groups already established, albeit for a few days or weeks. One Primary school believed that this was not best for the children so they turned this on its head, admitting summer born children first so that they could become established in a smaller group, before the older children joined them.

Some schools group the children to stagger the intake according to age, some according to friendships, others alphabetically according to their surnames. My view is that the more we can find out about our new intake before they attend the better. Then we can make informed decisions about groupings which will best support the children.

If a school is one form entry all of these children begin in the same class; however, if the school is larger the children will also be organised into classes. This is a logistical nightmare for schools to manage as they work through all the possible groupings. Again, the organisation of this differs from school to school. Some schools sort the classes on age using dates of birth, which then helps them to plan a gentler day for the youngest children, even incorporating naps if appropriate. Other schools group in order to achieve a mixed cohort, taking into account various categories such as age, English as an Additional Language (EAL), Special Educational Needs or Disability (SEND) and gender. Knowing as much as possible about the cohort helps to make this process easier. I found several schools in my research that arranged opportunities for parents and their children who were going to attend YR to meet informally, for example, providing an invitation tomeet for a picnic in a local park during the summer, which can help the children and parents to gel prior to starting school, or offering a couple of dates for an informal coffee and cake morning as a drop in for families.

As part of normal transition processes, most schools hold open evenings or sessions for parents to attend. These are information-sharing events and there is a huge discrepancy regarding what they contain and how these parents' sessions are organised. One school held an evening meeting in June and invited a couple of parents from their current YR class to attend. They found that new parents were happier asking other parents questions relating to uniform, lunches and trips amongst other things. Another school invited parents and children at the same time to a session when the classroom was set up and the children could play and the adults could talk. A large school invited both parents and children and while the children explored the EYFS area, the parents were receiving information about starting school. It is vital that parents have a clear understanding of the expectations for YR.

As discussed in Chapter 1, school readiness is a misleading term and many people mean different things when they talk about it. One group of schools got together and created an 'I can jigsaw' which they give to parents. This explains what they hope children will be able to do on entry to YR. Another school gave parents a 'super skills for school' chart. There are copies of these in Appendix A.

The idea of parents having something tangible to help to support their child is great, however, it comes with a health warning. There is a danger with all lists and charts that parents will put pressure on their children to perform and they just become a tick list. In addition, parents could feel overwhelmed and inadequate, particularly if their child cannot yet do many of the tasks listed. Perhaps this idea could be developed by sharing with parents that these 'I can' statements will be focused on in school during the Autumn term and if their child is ready and interested parents would be welcome to work on these at home over the summer. Parents need to know that all children develop and learn in different ways and at different rates and should be discouraged from comparing their child to others.

Home visits

An excellent way of finding out about the new cohort is to undertake home visits. Many schools are now choosing to do this, stating them as invaluable. In the home you get to see the child interacting on their turf. Mandy, a Reception class teacher I talked to, said, 'Seeing them at home is one of the best things so you can put a little bit of background and context to their experiences.' One parent shared her experience of home visits as being a life-line for her child.

> Noah had previously been attending a Special Needs Unit Nursery since the age of two and our first choice of school was a Special school. Unfortunately, due to the local demand for places, he was not allocated a place. We were particularly concerned about how he would settle into mainstream school and cope with a large class of Reception children. The teacher and teaching assistant visited Noah in our home, prior to his starting at school. The teaching assistant sat on the floor and played with Noah and by the end of the session, I remember

she was sitting wearing a cowboy hat and playing cars with him. This gave the class teacher a chance to talk to me and I was able to share my concerns. We discussed all sorts of issues like things that calm Noah down, ways to discipline him effectively and things that he can and can't do. I felt my worries (and there were a ton!) were heard and understood. I noticed that when Noah then attended the first taster session in the classroom he recognised the teaching assistant immediately which made this day far less traumatic for all of us. Home visits really made a difference for my child.

Conducting a home visit

Teachers need to plan ahead and agree a policy with regard to home visits. There are different timescales that schools follow for this and each school has its own idiosyncrasies. One school in North London had a transition week when children moved up to their next class teacher in July. This was a whole school policy and during this week the Reception teachers were able to undertake home visits. This particular school was fully committed to supporting transitions and had identified that it took several weeks for a class teacher to get to know the new class and learning was almost on hold while relationships were built. So they focused on transitions within the whole school and decided to dedicate a week to getting to know the new class, when the class teacher from the next year planned the current lessons for the week in conjunction with their current class teacher. Year 6 children spent this week partly visiting their secondary school and partly engaging in special activities. This week was the perfect opportunity for the Reception class teachers to visit the homes of the children due to start school in September.

A large Primary school in Surrey conducted their home visits in the autumn term over three days, before the Reception class children had begun. They chose to use this time as sometimes their cohort was not finalised until September and the time during the staggered intake was an ideal opportunity for the teacher and teaching assistant to visit the children's homes.

It is vital that home visits are written into school policies and that parents are informed that this is part of your transition arrangements for every child. In addition, some home visits may need to be arranged for outside the 'normal school day' as this can enable more parents to access a home visit. Such arrangements need to be agreed with senior management so that appropriate time off in lieu could be taken.

Schools need to know if a child in their new cohort has any additional needs, whether formally diagnosed or not. These children may need specific support with certain tasks and the home visit is the ideal time for a school to gather this information. Teachers can see, first hand, if the child uses any specialist equipment, or the way their home environment is organised for them, or if their parent needs to provide additional support for specific things.

Many schools used the home visit as an opportunity to talk through any paperwork with the family; however, I also met with several schools who insisted that home visits are not the time for paperwork. They felt that taking paperwork along can frighten or overwhelm families and that home visits are purely a chance to get to know the child and family better. This is a local decision, best made with knowledge of local families in mind.

If the family's first language is not English, we need to ensure that language does not become a large barrier to communication. One school used a *PenPal electronic pen* produced by Mantra Lingua[4] to translate key phrases into different languages. Another school tried to ensure that one of the members of staff who visited the home spoke a few words in the family's home language.

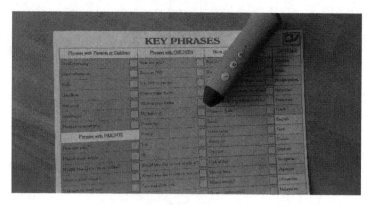

PenPal electronic pen

Another inner city school, which has on average 37 per cent of children with EAL, believed home visits to be essential. They shared with me some stories about home visits that highlighted the families need for additional support. One family lived with the curtains drawn shut and the child appeared fatigued and withdrawn. His milk teeth were not fully formed and his mother did not want to take him to the dentist. The teacher suspected a vitamin D deficiency and was able to talk to the family about the importance of fresh air and sunshine. She put the family in touch with a health visitor who was able to support them further.

Another anecdote shared was about a family who had put in a request for their child to start straight into Year 1 as he was born in early September and appeared to be exceptionally clever. Indeed he was a bright child, however when the teacher met him, she found him still wearing a nappy. Both parents were well educated and travelled the world for their jobs, frequently taking him with them. It was more convenient for them if he wore a nappy while they travelled. Their home had very few toys but many artefacts and things collected from their travels. During the home visit, it was clear that the child did not know how to play and needed lots of guidance. The teacher was able to offer advice on toilet training, share the benefits of learning through play for a child of his age and ability, and suggest that Year 1 may not be the best place for him, as the school wanted him to develop holistically. Once in Reception, he thrived and relished the opportunities to play and develop socially.

TOP TIPS FOR A SUCCESSFUL HOME VISIT

- Ensure that two adults attend – one to focus on the child, the other to focus on the parents.

- Try to keep the session informal as this will be less threatening for the family.

- Keep it short – 15 to 20 minutes will suffice.

- Ensure you are respectful at all times; you are a visitor in their home.

- Offer to take off your shoes on entry.

- Take a few toys to help to engage the child.

- Perhaps read a short story to the child.

- Share photos of the school and members of staff with the child to talk about their new school.

- Ask the child if they want to share their favourite toy or show you anything.

- Try to establish the child's interests and fascinations.

- Share the routine of the school day, reiterating start times and pick up times.

- Try to check parent's understanding of any intake arrangements, for example knowing when and where their child should attend.

- Allow time for questions.

- Take the lead from the parents to address all of their concerns.

- Ask if there is anything happening in their family that the school need to know, for instance a new baby, a parent starting at college, new job and so on.

- If a parent insists that they do not want a home visit, try to arrange to meet with them at an alternative venue, at school, nursery or in a children's centre, so that you have the opportunity to meet the child with their parent. If possible, this should be a place that is familiar to the child.

The role of the adult in YR

Another issue for children entering Primary school for the first time is the difference in adult-child ratios between nursery and school. A child can be attending a nursery setting and have one adult for every six to eight children and literally the next day attend school where they could have anything from 1:15 to 1:30 adults to children! In England there are regulations limiting the size of infant classes (including YR) to 30 pupils per teacher, however, the majority of YR classes also employ a teaching assistant thus making the adult-child ratio smaller. A child will notice this ratio decreasing as they will undoubtedly receive less adult attention during the school day than they have had before in any settings they have attended or at home.

A primary role of the teacher is to create stimulating and engaging learning environments within their classrooms which is a strength of the Reggio Emilia approach. Whilst on a study tour visiting several preschools in Reggio Emilia, I observed that they refer to the learning environment as the third teacher. They have two main adults working with the children, the Pedagogista who is the educational teacher and the Atelierista who is the creative director or artist. The environment is referred to as the third teacher because the children can learn so much through interacting with it. For example, we can provide children with many open-ended resources so that they can imagine and create their own stories. The way we present materials to children should make them want to dive in and get involved.

As mentioned in Chapter 5, we can set up invitations to learn when we tap into children's natural curiosity and intrigue to encourage them to engage with the resources. After an icy spell, when the children had found some ice in a builder's tray in the outside area, the teacher provided them with some tools and ice blocks, some containing minibeast models, both inside and outside to explore further.

Many teachers are enjoying inventing imaginative scenarios for their children to engage with. For example, after a forest schools session, one teacher created some salt-dough 'eggs' which she put in the ashes of the fire for the children to find during their next forest school session. The children found these 'eggs' and decided that they were dinosaur eggs. They made nests for them, choosing materials that would keep the eggs warm. After a couple of weeks, cracks appeared on the 'dinosaur eggs' which intrigued the children further. At a later date, the dinosaurs 'hatched' and wreaked havoc in the headteacher's office, much to the children's delight! After the initial provocation, the teachers followed the children's lead in extending and developing their play. They created an archaeological dig in the outside area, created a museum for their finds and did lots of research on the Internet and in books about dinosaurs and fossils.

Another YR class arranged for their children to arrive one morning to find dinosaur footprints in the playground. The children wondered how they had appeared and if they had been visited by a dinosaur overnight. You can imagine the excitement of the children that day! They remained focused on finding clues about the dinosaurs and engaged in mathematics as they measured the prints and counted how many there were. Some children wrote a letter to the dinosaur to leave in the classroom that night, drawing on their emerging literacy skills whilst most children talked non-stop about the visitor! It is really important that we link these wonderful ideas with learning and the EYFS to ensure that we are engaging in meaningful activities.

The role of the adult in YR is also to build positive relationships with both the parents and children (see Chapter 10). Schools need to identify the children's key person quickly and inform the family at the home visit or during the transition arrangements. Families need to know who to talk to and it is very useful to have a named contact as early as possible. Children can be provided with a photo of that practitioner so that they also know who they are. One school created photo books containing these photographs and additional photos of the YR learning environment and playground (see Figure 8.1) which they shared with their new intake the term before they started at school.

My new school

We take books home in a bag like this.

This is our school field.

When we are in school we keep our book bag in our tray with our name on.

There are two classrooms for Reception children called Rabbits and Hedgehogs.

This is the big playground. We play with our friends here at break time and lunch time.

We have our own toilets.

Figure 8.1 Example of a photo book given to children

In order to get to know the children, it will also help if teachers invest in building relationships with the various nursery and preschool settings that feed their schools. Schools need to take on this responsibility themselves. I have heard many teachers say that they find it hard to engage with settings because they have so many that feed them, however in the interests of the children we must find a way forward.

One school in central London visited every nursery or preschool that had more than a couple of children feeding their school. They used the transition week in the summer term when their own classes were moving on up to Year 1. This was the ideal time to pop into the nursery schools to see the children in their new cohort. Where schools were locally arranged in clusters, some schools and settings jointly held transition events as part of these clusters. This is also an opportunity to find out from the children's current key person the things that are useful to know but rarely written down.

One school used some of their Pupil Premium money to increase adult ratios in YR during the first term by funding additional teaching assistants to work with specific groups of children. Another school used some funding to deliver specific intervention programmes, aimed at developing children's social and emotional skills, and yet another paid for some training for the whole EYFS staff on specialist behavioural support.

Becoming a children-ready school

I love this quote from Mike Huber:[5]

> We need to ask ourselves, is our school ready to support children with the social skills they have and help them develop more skills? Is our school ready to give children the time, space, and materials they need to explore and discover?

Many schools attempt to make the transition into Reception as smooth as possible and consider the move from the child's perspective. They are able to gather information about the children and family prior to starting, create a learning environment that is aimed at the interests and needs of the new children and offer information to parents and children as part of the preparation process. However in her book about starting school, Liz Booker[6] argues that for some children, learning how to be at school actually requires them to learn to be a different person altogether. School requires a child to interact, act and react in ways that could be alien to them prior to starting. Some people have even suggested that schools are institutionalising children, therefore we need to be sensitive to this and try to accept children as they are, without expecting them to fit into this school-shaped mould.

One of my aims as an author is to encourage practitioners to review their practice in the light of the issues raised. To further support adults in this task I have included some self-evaluation questions in the appendices. Appendix C is aimed at adults working in schools and consists of several questions which can be discussed as a whole team, allowing practitioners to identify their strengths but also areas that they want to develop in order to benefit the children.

Here are some ideas for how to be children-ready:

- Find out as much as you can about your new cohort: undertake home visits, build relationships with your main feeder settings and plan to meet the children and their families several times prior to starting full time.

- Trust the information shared by early years settings – they know their children very well. Remember that most children will regress slightly on transition and after a long break and this does not mean that the transfer information was inaccurate.

- Invite local settings to story time sessions and to watch school productions or nativity plays.

- Provide a welcoming environment and increase your adult-child ratios for the autumn term.

- Include all adults who will work with the children in any training sessions, for example teachers, teaching assistants, mid-day supervisors, students and ensure that all adults understand the unique role that YR plays within the school.

- Review school policies in the light of very young children and individual differences, for example allow flexibility on uniform issues or a unisex uniform, or allow transitional objects to support children to settle in.

- Accept each child as they are and ensure that they know that they are valued and loved.

- Accept behavioural differences between children and understand that YR expectations need to be adjusted for age and stage of development.

- Attend training on issues such as high anxiety, autism, gender confusion, dyspraxia and communication and language disorders and keep early identification high on the agenda.

- Keep children's interests and fascinations central to your activities, resources and learning environment.

- Prior to any sedentary activities engage in some very physical activity.

- Allow plenty of time for playing and exploring and active learning.

- Create an ethos that values attitudes to learning and thinking.

- Maintain a consistent routine and share a visual timetable with the children.

- Introduce children to school routines gradually over the year, for example playtime in the large playground and assemblies.

- Keep everything active with short teaching sessions and have lots of wriggle time! Include songs like 'Move like me' or 'Shake your sillies out.'

- Make story times interactive with props/actions/puppets/voices and pictures.

- Invite parents from your current Reception year to attend a new parents' evening/session to alleviate concerns.

- Allocate a class representative for other parents to be in touch with – if possible choose an experienced parent who has children higher up in the school.

- Invite the new children to draw or paint a picture on their visit in the Summer term and display these in September to help welcome the children.

- Pair up the new children with buddies from older year groups to look after them when introducing whole school playtimes.

- Provide plenty of time for several settling in sessions for the children; include tours of the school, where to put their coat, visits to the toilets and hall and so on.

- Ensure that children experience all elements of the school day prior to starting, including lunchtime and playtime.

- Plan in some 1:1 time with each new child and value their uniqueness!

I thought I'd give the last word in this chapter to the children themselves. I asked several children for their top tips for teachers who are going to help new children settle into school life. I have recorded children's words verbatim for full impact!

TOP TIPS FOR TEACHERS

- Make sure lessons are fun and happy.

- Give the children good advice like what to do when the bell rings.

- Tell them it doesn't matter if they can read or write or not because that's what they'll learn.

- Be really encouraging.

- Give them time to rest and sometimes listen to relaxing music and let them take deep breaths in and deep breaths out.

- Read books to them.

- Be nice and be kind and make them feel at home and be fun and good and helpful.

- Share cuddles and help us little ones as it is a little scary as my mummy and daddy and nanny cannot come with me.

So as we focus on schools being ready for the children they serve, take a tip from the children themselves: remember it can be scary for the little ones as their mummies and daddies cannot attend school with them, so share cuddles and breathe!

REFLECTIVE PRACTICE QUESTIONS

1. How can we ensure that we are ready for children and not expecting children to be ready for school?

2. When do you feel is the optimum time for home visits? What can you learn from a home visit that you cannot learn elsewhere?

3. How can we foster a love of learning in the children in our care?

Notes

1. Schleicher, A. (2017) In Gaunt, C. 'OECD in "schoolification" warning.' *Nursery World*, 26 June – 9 July, 2017, p.6.
2. OECD (2017) *Starting Strong 2017: Key OECD Indicators on Early Childhood Education and Care*. Retrieved from www.oecd.org/edu/starting-strong-2017-9789264276116-en.htm, on 5 October 2017.
3. Early Excellence (2017) *Teaching Four and Five Year Olds: The Hundred Review of the Reception Year in England*. Retrieved from http://earlyexcellence.com/hundredreview, on 9 October 2017, p.4.

4. See http://uk.mantralingua.com/product/penpal.
5. Huber, M. (2017) *Embracing Rough and Tumble Play: Teaching with the Body in Mind.* St Paul, MN: Redleaf Press, p.22.
6. Booker, L. (2002) *Starting School: Young Children Learning Cultures.* Buckingham: Open University Press.

9

Settings Supporting Children

CHAPTER OBJECTIVE

This chapter will focus on how early years settings support children to move on to school. It will offer practical ideas for settings and schools to implement as well as cameos and case studies outlining effective practice and the positive impact different strategies have had on children during this phase.

Early years settings are on the frontline when it comes to supporting children to be school ready. In England, three- and four-year-olds are entitled to free childcare and according to the National Audit Office[1] there is 'almost universal take-up of hours offered to parents'. The majority of these children attend Private, Voluntary and Independent (PVI) settings and transfer on to maintained schools for YR.

This chapter will share some effective practice relating to transitions and what settings can do to enable children to transfer to school smoothly. It considers how we teach children to be independent, manage their feelings and behaviour and foster the Characteristics of Effective Learning (CoEL). It also discusses how settings and schools need to collaborate in order to better support children.

Supporting children

Settings support children as they prepare for school emotionally as well as physically. We can plan in specific time and space to focus on listening to children and ask how they feel about attending school, giving them the opportunity to tell us their thoughts, feelings, worries and fears and also to share their excitement. We can use pictures or objects as a starting point for discussion, for example, bringing in a school book bag, or sharing some photos of one of the schools children will attend. It is important not to over emphasise when talking about 'big school' or what it will be like. For some children attending school can be built up into a huge mountain which can overwhelm them and for others, when they go to school, it doesn't live up to their pre-conceived ideas and they become disappointed!

Many settings set up a role play area for children to play at schools. We can provide them with school uniform to dress up in, lunch boxes, school bags, pencils and paper for drawing and writing, tables and chairs for desks and whiteboards with markers to encourage children to mark-make. We can also play alongside children but should avoid the temptation of being too authoritative or exaggerating the role if we end up role playing the teacher!

One lovely way to discuss school with children is to read stories relating to school. There are several stories on the market, some of which are about children starting school for the first time. Others are general stories within the context of school. In addition, we can tell children stories which will support them with different aspects such as developing friendships, all of which will help them when they start school. Appendix E lists some key books that can be used with children prior to starting school.

An additional role for settings in supporting children prior to starting school lies in them supporting the parents. The importance of engaging with parents is discussed fully in Chapter 10. In settings we have already worked hard to build up successful relationships with families and can use these to further support them during this transitional phase. Parents may prefer to ask us questions relating to school, rather than ask the school, and we can remind parents when the transition meetings for their child's school are and encourage them to attend.

Supporting children to be independent learners

The more independent we can enable our children to become, the more they will adapt to being in a school situation. Being independent allows children to make choices and take their learning forward at their own pace and not rely on an adult to help. It is also about children who can manage their own hygiene and dress and undress by themselves. As mentioned in Chapter 1, almost all respondents to my survey on school readiness believed that children who were ready for school excelled in self-care skills. We can support children to develop these skills by offering them opportunities to dress and undress, practise changing for physical sessions into shorts and t-shirts and dress and undress dolls and teddies. Some settings have purchased or created fastenings boards which have a variety of buttons, zips, Velcro and other fastenings for the children to practise using. We can also encourage children to put on their own shoes, coats and wellington boots. Teach strategies for children to use, for example, to lay their coat upside down on the floor, place their arms into the coat and lift their arms up and backwards which brings the coat over their head and into place.

It is also helpful if we support children with activities which will improve their fine motor skills; however, we must bear in mind that gross motor skills develop first and it is vital to ensure that they are developed before we worry too much about their fine motor skills. Children need both hand-eye coordination and fine motor control to complete tasks such as writing, using a knife and fork, using scissors, throwing and catching, threading and lacing and so on. Children's fine motor skills are still developing until they are around nine years old which is why their handwriting tends to be rather large until around the end of Year Three.

Many settings incorporate elements of the school day or routine which encourage independence, for example, using a self-registration system whereby on arrival, the children find their name and stick it on a board. One setting stuck labels onto large bricks and as the children entered, they found their named brick and began to build a wall. By the time everyone had arrived for the day they had built a small wall.

Other ways that settings encourage children to be independent include: ensuring that resources, boxes and drawers are labelled with pictures and words; organising resources so that they are accessible to the children; providing photo instructions for tasks like handwashing; and providing dressing-up clothes with easy fasteners. We can also offer children choices about which resources they need and teach them how to use tools like scissors, paint brushes and a dustpan and brush, to name a few.

Managing feelings and behaviour

Children experience a range of big emotions and do not always understand how to deal with them. It is helpful to put this in the context of what happens in our brains during stressful situations. When we experience something the information moves from our senses to the *thalamus*, which acts like an air traffic controller, usually sending the information on to the thinking part of our brain called the *cerebrum*, which passes the information on to other parts of the brain, including the *amygdala*, which translates it into emotions and action. When we are feeling stressed or in a conflict situation, it is as if our thalamus decides that we don't have time to think about the situation and need to act immediately to remove the threat or get away from the danger, sending the information straight to the amygdala. This is when we have what is known as the freeze, fight or flight response. Dan Goleman[2] calls this 'the amygdala hijacking' as our bodies have a physiological response with increased adrenalin to enable us to run away or put up a fight. As adults we find ways to cope with this response, sometimes simply saying to ourselves, 'Don't rise to it...' or 'Just walk away!' Children have not yet learned what to do when they go into freeze, fight or flight mode. We need to teach them calming strategies and how to respond when they have these big feelings.

TOP 5 CALMING STRATEGIES

1. Acknowledge feelings and name them – I can see you are cross/upset...

2. Teach children breathing exercises to help to maintain their normal state again, for example pretending to blow out birthday candles, blowing up pretend balloons, huffing and puffing – dragon breath!

3. Slowly count to 10 together or sing a nursery rhyme. This will require children to breathe regularly and in a rhythm.

4. Copy rhythmic actions – rocking, walking, swinging, stretching up high to down low and so on. It is the motion and rhythm that help.

5. Dim the lights, limit noise in the room, play some soft and slow music, or play calm games like sleeping lions as all these can help to create a calm atmosphere.

Once children are calm we may be able to talk with them about their behaviour. During a tantrum is not the best time to talk! If the children have fought over a toy or resource and we need to resolve the argument, we can use a technique called the HighScope problem-solving approach,[3] which changes any negative issue or conflict into a positive opportunity to problem solve. It follows six steps and comes highly recommended.

THE PROBLEM-SOLVING APPROACH TO CONFLICT RESOLUTION

1. Approach calmly

   - Place yourself at the child's level.

   - Use a calm voice and a gentle touch.

- If the children are arguing over a toy, all hold the toy together to stop the tug-of-war and allow all parties to still feel in control.

2. Acknowledge children's feelings

    - Name and describe the children's feelings, for example 'Jane you look cross and Nigel you look upset.'

    - Avoid asking questions until children are calmer.

3. Gather information

    - Observe children's actions and describe the problem or ask 'what?' questions to find out what happened.

4. Restate the problem

    - Repeat again the information you have observed or heard and check that your understanding of the problem is correct. 'So, Jane was using the pushchair and Nigel came along and really wanted to use the pushchair too?'

    - Present it to children as a problem. 'We have a problem! We only have one pushchair and two children want to use it. What should we do?'

5. Ask for ideas for solutions and choose one together

    - Ask the children for ideas, encourage negotiation and agreements.

    - You may need to model potential solutions until children understand the process and are able to contribute their own ideas.

- Other children may have gathered to watch the drama unfold; ask them to contribute as all ideas are welcome and should be valued.

- Encourage the children to choose an idea that will work and ensure that all children understand the solution.

6. Be prepared to give follow-up support

- Stay nearby to support the solution, for instance if you are using a sand timer ensure that when the sand has run through, you are there to monitor the swapping over.

- Tell the children, 'You solved the problem!'

(Adapted from HighScope Educational Research Foundation[3])

To share is an abstract concept and does not usually come naturally to adults, let alone children. On my courses I tend to provide learners with a small bowl of sweets to keep them going throughout the day. I then ask them to think of as many different ways as possible that we could share the sweets. For example, we could pass the bowl around and all take a few, we could divide them equally or we could only share them with our friends... To share can mean any number of things and the concept of sharing requires explanation. Being able to share and play alongside children amicably is a useful skill when going to school so they need to be taught to share and take turns just as they are taught other skills.

We can model sharing and use the language associated with it, such as, take turns, play together, one at a time, divide, same amount and so on. We must also ensure that we acknowledge and praise sharing or taking turns, labelling the praise and talking through what children are doing so that they feel good about sharing with each other. Planning specific activities which directly promote these skills can really help, for example turn-taking games, group activities, art/craft when we need to share resources. When children find it difficult to share an object or toy, we can use the problem-solving approach to resolve this conflict, turning the issue into a learning opportunity for everyone.

Above all, we need to have realistic expectations about our children. They will not always share and we need to accept this whilst providing them with opportunities to play alongside others and practise sharing. Sometimes a child will not want to share. We must respect this, yet try to explain how this might make their friends feel. Toys are not that important to us as adults, but to children they are the most valuable thing in the world. If I had my most valuable possession with me, I certainly wouldn't want to share it with others!

The ethos we create in our settings also supports children's emotional and behavioural development. We need to be accepting of children. Even if we do not always like their behaviour, children need to be in no doubt that we like them as a person. One setting shared a story with me about a child who was hurt in the outside area. They didn't have much language and the practitioner was trying to ascertain what had happened, so she asked the other children. They all replied, 'I didn't do it!' This indicates they live in a culture of blame. In their lives they know that there are different expectations of them depending on whether or not they are guilty/not guilty. When the practitioner explained that she didn't want to tell anyone off, she just needed to know what had happened so that she could keep them safe and make sure it didn't happen again, one child owned up. With a big sigh, he said, 'OK then, I did it!' This little boy was able to think about the situation and what had happened and felt able to talk about the incident because any accusations and blame were removed.

In another setting a little girl was crying and asking for her mummy. When her practitioner investigated further, she had emptied out a container of lolly sticks onto the floor and was worried that she would get into trouble.

Her practitioner said, 'Thank you so much, I wanted you to use them and now we can see all of the colours much more easily.' The girl happily played for the rest of the session and I am sure that the response of the practitioner will have helped her to feel accepted in the setting and understand that it is OK to make mistakes.

When we support children to understand their feelings and get in touch with their emotions, it is often referred to as developing their *emotional intelligence*. This is about helping children to be aware of their feelings, having empathy towards others and learning strategies that they can use to manage their emotions. These are difficult skills for a three- or four-year-old to master – I even know some adults who struggle with this! This links closely with fostering the CoEL.

Promoting the Characteristics of Effective Learning

Settings need to foster the CoEL in the children in their care. Previous chapters have shared ideas about children who are displaying these characteristics.

Many teachers, practitioners and educationalists agree that school readiness is not about academic skills like reading and writing. These skills can easily be taught once a child has settled into school and is ready. Readiness for this learning will differ from child to child. However, during research I have encountered many examples of children who are interested in reading, writing and other more academic skills. We would do the children a disservice if we did not build on this interest.

Jack (3 years) had been showing an interest in reading, listening to stories and drawing. He attended a forest school nursery and had recently been picking up sticks and mark-making, not attempting letters but drawing recognisable pictures. During a cookery session he wanted to put his baked goods on a side of the oven, so his practitioner gave him a sheet of foil and said, 'Ok, I will write your name for you and we will put it on the oven.' He replied, 'No, I will do it.' He clearly wrote Jack as his first attempt at writing!

Jack was ready to learn. His setting had scaffolded his learning by providing him with opportunities to mark-make and listen to stories, yet had avoided pushing him into reading or writing. Jack already saw himself as a writer which would stand him in good stead for the future. In settings we need to focus on Phase One[4] of 'Letters and Sounds' and resist the temptation to go beyond this. Phase One includes oral blending and segmenting so there are plenty of opportunities for us to stretch and challenge more able children during this phase.

In another setting, some nettles were growing in a natural area in their outdoor space. Rather than dig them out, the practitioners recognised this as an opportunity for children to risk assess for themselves. They spoke to the children about the problem that the nettles posed and asked them how they could solve the problem. After some discussion, the children decided that they needed a sign warning people about the nettles. So they took a photograph of the nettles and, with some help from the practitioners, made a sign to warn others. These children were ready to learn; they were demonstrating qualities that would ease their transition into school.

This is a nettle.
It can hurt you.

During my research I also came across a three-and-a-half-year-old girl who, after reading *The Day the Crayons Quit* by Drew Daywalt,[5] wanted to do her own investigation. She wondered what would happen if she used a pink crayon on pink paper. She found some pink paper and made lots of marks with various media including paint, crayons and pens. In addition to using pink paper, she also compared it with white paper and looked at the differences. The practitioners assisted her in her learning, making sure that she was able to access the resources she needed. She was ready to learn and displaying a 'can do' attitude throughout her investigation. She is due to move on to YR in September and the nursery intends to share this information with her new school.

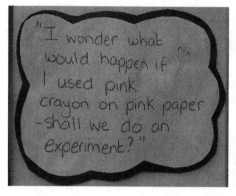

Settings and schools working collaboratively

Those of us working in early years have known how important it is for settings and schools to work collaboratively in order to support the child in their transition from one to another. However, we also know how difficult this task is. It is not as simple as it sounds.

CASE STUDY 1

A small preschool (20 children on roll) is located in the village hall a few hundred yards from the village Primary school. For the past few years all the children, bar one or two, have moved on to this school (around 10 children each year). The preschool is open from 9.15am until 12.15pm and has four members of staff with a fifth available to cover occasionally. Despite being situated close to the school, the preschool staff and teachers rarely see each other. The school invites the preschool to watch their Christmas production dress rehearsal each year. The preschool leader stated, 'We know the teacher at the school, however we can't really collaborate more because we are only open in the mornings. I think the teacher wants the children to be able to write their name so we work hard at that with the children.'

CASE STUDY 2

A medium-sized nursery setting offers full day care between 8am and 6pm. They are located in the suburbs of a city. The nursery has approximately 24 children who move on to school each year and usually feeds about 11 different Primary schools. They state, 'Working together with the schools is an impossible task as we feed so many. We have tried to get in touch with teachers in the past without much success. We really should try again. We just do our best to prepare the children for school in the way we feel is best for them.'

CASE STUDY 3

A large nursery offers full day care for children aged from three months to five years and after school care for children aged up to eight years. The nursery has approximately 35 children who go on to school each year and they tend to go to over 15 different Primary schools. There are two main Primaries that a lot of the children go to which are closest to the nursery in terms of location, however many staff appear to have a negative view of their local schools with regard to transition. One practitioner stated, 'The schools always disregard our observations and I don't think they even read the profiles we send across. All that hard work for nothing.' After trying to make contact with one of the schools a young practitioner said, 'I don't feel confident to talk to the teacher as I only have a Level 2 qualification.'

These settings are in very different circumstances yet none of them feel they are successfully collaborating with local

Primary schools. In order to share ideas of how settings and schools have successfully managed this, I want to look at how we can overcome some of the issues involved. We all have different *cognitive frames* that influence how we think, feel and behave in relation to a specific issue. For example, time frames set the deadlines within which we work. Sometimes our frames limit our thinking and become barriers to partnership working. Table 9.1 considers various barriers highlighted by the case studies above and shares possible solutions.

We must ensure that we provide accurate assessment information about the children moving on to school. Many settings I visited had approached their feeder schools and asked them exactly how much information they wanted to receive. In almost all cases it was less than they were giving, thus cutting down on paperwork for the settings to complete. Several settings and a few local authorities had devised a specific 'moving on' form or 'transfer information sheet' for settings to complete about each child. These forms were created in groups consisting of both school and setting staff and reflected the needs of the locality in addition to providing information on the Prime Areas and CoEL.

It is also vital that we pass on to schools any information regarding children's SEND. As mentioned in Chapter 7, if we have any concerns at all about a child's development, the earlier we can intervene the better. So we must discuss our concerns with parents and continue to observe, perhaps inviting an expert to observe alongside us. Our concerns, however small or seemingly insignificant, must be shared as part of the information we pass on to school.

There are many ways that we can promote strong school-setting relationships. Here is a list gathered from talking to several different providers about their practice:

- Frequent visits to school/setting to build relationships.

- Joint teacher/practitioner moderation of judgements and entry assessments when children start school.
- Joint teacher/practitioner observations in setting prior to starting school.
- Sharing information between school/setting with each other and with parents.
- Close links with schools, for example visit to watch dress rehearsal of Christmas Nativities.
- Joint events, for example summer teddy bears picnic.
- Joint school readiness workshops for parents.
- Joint summer holiday play sessions, school and preschool.
- Invite teachers to visit settings and ask to visit schools.
- Share resources together, for instance dual language books to support specific children.
- Invite teachers to attend setting sports day or leaving ceremonies.
- Maintain links through cluster meetings, taking it in turns to host.

An excellent way to ensure that we are supporting children as fully as possible is to review our practice. I have developed a self-evaluation tool (see Appendix D) aimed at assisting practitioners in reviewing and evaluating their practice. When we home in on the child and their individual needs, teaching them to develop those CoEL, we better support them in their transition to school.

Table 9.1 Case study barriers with possible solutions

Barrier	Type of thinking	Example	Solution
Attitudes like 'That won't work here' or 'I can't'	Impossibility	Case study 1 – 'We can't really collaborate more because...' Case study 2 – 'Working together with the schools is an impossible task...'	Can't implies never, which is untrue; although the task may be difficult it is not impossible and we need to ensure that we work on the parts of the situation that we can influence and are possible
Setting feeds too many schools	Overwhelming	Case study 2 – 'We feed so many (schools)...'	Break task down into smaller steps: 1. Write a list of the schools you feed 2. Prioritise them re children causing concern, number of children attending that school, etc. 3. Contact the schools in your priority order 4. Invite the teacher to visit the nursery at a time when the child/ren will be there, including during and out of school hours
Making assumptions about what schools want in terms of children being ready and making generalisations about teachers and schools	Assuming and generalising	Case study 1 – 'I think the teacher wants...' Case study 3 – 'I don't think they (teachers) even read the profiles...' Case study 3 – 'The schools always disregard our observations...'	It is important not to make assumptions or generalise about what schools want or what they do. We must however ensure that these ideas are based on fact not hearsay or figments of our imagination. Contact your main feeder schools and ask the question, 'What do you want us to focus on with our school leavers?' If too many to approach, ask a few. Also ask about the information that you send on to school. Is it too much or not enough? Does it answer the things that the schools really want to know? Perhaps you are sending on too much information – imagine if you had 30 learning journals to read in your summer holiday... A short summary will suffice

cont.

Barrier	Type of thinking	Example	Solution
Comparing qualifications can make you feel inadequate or lacking in confidence	Inadequacy	Case study 3 – 'I don't feel qualified to talk to the teacher as I only have a Level 2 qualification…'	Other than the parent you are the best qualified to talk about your key children when discussing their transition into school. It's not about paper qualifications, it's about knowing the children really well and helping a colleague (teacher) to plan for their future learning. Be confident in yourself and secure in your knowledge about the children
When you've tried to collaborate in the past and don't feel you have got anywhere	Resignation	Case study 2 – 'We have tried to get in touch with teachers in the past without much success…'	Don't give up! Persevere and demonstrate those CoEL that we are hoping the children will foster! Staffing and priorities in schools change; you may find the school is now ready to collaborate. If you have concerns about a specific child that will attend, explain this and try to bypass the receptionist or secretary. Go straight to the SENCO or YR teacher themselves
When the to-do list is too long and although we want to collaborate, time runs out	Good intentions	Case study 2 – 'We really should try again…'	Everyone wakes up in the morning wanting to do the best they can. It is important not to beat yourself up about not having time to do all that you want to do, or leaving things on the back burner because you do the best for the children in your care. Each cohort that moves onto school only has one shot at transition therefore we must ensure that they have the best opportunities to settle in quickly. Part of our role in settings is to ensure that we collaborate with schools to make this happen, so there's no time like the present – contact them today!

REFLECTIVE PRACTICE QUESTIONS

1. How do you encourage children to become independent learners?

2. What do we need to do to ensure the potential of collaborative working between setting and school is achieved?

3. How do we create opportunities for children to be present, feel involved and take some control of the transition into school?

Notes

1. National Audit Office (2016) Entitlement to free early education and childcare report HC853, 2 March 2016. Retrieved from https://www.nao.org.uk/wp-content/uploads/2016/03/Entitlement-to-free-early-education-and-childcare-Summary.pdf, on 9 October 2017.
2. Goleman, D. (2006) *Emotional Intelligence: Why It Can Matter More Than IQ*. New York: Bantam Books.
3. HighScope Educational Research Foundation (2017) How does High/scope help children learn how to resolve conflicts? Retrieved from https://highscope.org/faq, on 9 October 2017.
4. DCSF (2008) *Letters and Sounds: Principles and Practice of High Quality Phonics. Phase One Teaching Programme*. Retrieved from https://www.gov.uk/government/publications/letters-and-sounds-principles-and-practice-of-high-quality-phonics-phase-one-teaching-programme, on 9 October 2017.
5. Daywalt, D. (2014) *The Day the Crayons Quit*. London: Harper Collins.

10

Engaging Parents and Carers

CHAPTER OBJECTIVE

This chapter will highlight the importance of engaging with parents and will offer ideas for how to strengthen these relationships. It will share real case studies of settings and schools working in partnership as examples of effective practice.

Partnership with parents is a phrase that has been used for many years, alongside the mantra that parents are the child's first educator. What do we mean when we use these phrases? Are we just paying lip service to the invaluable contribution that parents can make to our schools and settings? Of course parents will be educating their children, mostly due to the fact that children learn a vast amount through imitation. However, do parents want to be called educators and do educators get a little precious when the term is used to describe parents?

The Rumbold report[1] in 1990 appears to be the first formal document to mention 'parent partnership' and this term has since been widely used. The early years sector knows it needs to work with parents and doing so will enhance their practice, however, partnership may not be the best term to use. Sometimes parents feel unable to be full partners as they are working long hours or have little time to invest in the partnership, therefore instead Goodall and Montgomery[2] talk about 'parental engagement'. This is about parents being involved in what the child is doing and remaining interested in their children's learning, even if they are unable to visit the setting; thus they are still engaging with the learning.

For the purposes of this chapter I refer to parental engagement and use the term parent to mean parent, carer or anyone with parental responsibility for the child. This chapter considers how we engage with parents over the issue of school readiness. It will share examples from settings and offer practical ideas for how to fully engage parents.

Parental involvement and parental engagement

Children begin learning in the womb and when they are born their parents are their first teachers. A child's family and home environment has a strong impact on their language and literacy development and educational achievement. This impact is stronger during the child's early years but continues throughout their school years. The EPPE research[3] has shown that parental involvement in children's education from an early age has a significant effect on educational achievement, and continues to do so into adolescence and adulthood.

The Oxford English dictionary definition of to involve[4] is to 'include (something) as a necessary part' whereas the Oxford English dictionary definition of to engage[5] is 'establish a meaningful contact or connection with'. Although subtle, there is a difference. Involving parents could be something we feel obliged to do to tick the box, or something that happens to parents, for example, telling parents how they can get involved with us. Engaging with parents is a more meaningful enterprise and one which will impact on both parties, for example, listening to how parents could contribute and finding out what their needs are.

Goodall and Montgomery[6] sum up this idea as a 'shift in emphasis, away from the relationship between parents and schools, to a focus on the relationship between parents and their children's learning'. This focus on learning also reflects the change that has gradually happened in our settings where we stop thinking in terms of what children are doing but rather focus on what and how children are learning. This links closely with the Characteristics of Effective Learning (CoEL) and discussing these is a useful way to refocus when talking to parents about their children's learning.

Our view of parents and their interactions with our settings matter and will influence how successful we are with engaging parents. For example, I have heard practitioners say, 'The parents don't bother us much here' or 'We struggle to get enough parent volunteers to fundraise for us.' These attitudes both have underlying tones that imply that parents are not viewed as an active part of the setting; they have their uses, for example, to aid fundraising, but other than that we prefer them to leave us alone! It is a useful exercise to review our attitudes towards parents and think about how we can better engage with them in a more meaningful way.

We can, of course, both involve and engage parents and therefore have the best of both worlds! It appears that the majority of research[7] confirms that the more interested, involved and engaged parents are the better children will fare academically. Where parents have high aspirations for their children and participate in things like conversation, reading and play, this has a positive impact on children's development and education.[8]

Our influence on the home learning environment (HLE)

If parents have such a huge impact on children's learning and development, we should ensure that we are positively influencing them. Many settings are offering parents advice about how to help their children at home, or ideas relating to fun activities they could try together with their child. Such ideas will support children as they move on to school.

The Provider Influence on the HLE research study[9] was commissioned by the Department for Children, Schools and Families in 2010 and looked at the effectiveness of strategies used by settings to support parents aiming to give their child the best start in early home learning. It used the seven elements from the Early Home Learning Environment Index to define home learning. However, it found that parents referred to a broader range of activities than the index represented. For example, parents also included learning through play, helping with domestic chores, riding bikes, sports sessions and outdoor activities as important home learning activities. I would agree; children learn in so many different contexts, it is difficult to confine home learning to just seven activities.

EARLY HOME LEARNING ENVIRONMENT INDEX[10]

1. Parent reading to the child.

2. Parent taking their child to the library.

3. Child playing with letters.

4. Parent helping their child to learn the alphabet.

5. Parent teaching their child numbers or counting.

6. Parent teaching their child songs, poems or nursery rhymes.

7. Child painting or drawing at home.

This report outlined the ways that practitioners can engage parents whilst highlighting the pressures on parents that groups need to support. For example, time was identified as a constraint to the amount of home learning activities undertaken, older siblings were identified as leading many home learning activities and families where no adult works full time were identified as needing additional support as this group appeared to do less home learning. They found that 61 per cent of parents attended an event after receiving a funded place, for example stay and play, and of these 97 per cent tried home learning activities suggested at these events. In terms of settings, 81 per cent gave examples of positive impact on levels of early home learning by engaging with parents. The methods frequently discussed were providing activities for parents to do at home, talking with parents and showing them how to do early learning activities with their children.

The report also considered confidence levels about engaging parents in early home learning and found 41 per cent of early years staff felt very confident and 38 per cent felt quite confident. Therefore this implies that the majority of staff in a setting feel able to engage parents in home learning; however, the report identified that a third of staff feel their training and information needs about early home learning were not being met.

Engaging parents in home learning does not have to be complicated. Rhymes are the perfect way to engage with parents. We can invite parents in to share their favourite rhymes and ask those who have English as an additional language to teach us some in their home language. We can even set up a lending library between home and the setting, so that parents can borrow a rhyme bag or rhyme book to use with their child at home. This could become a reciprocal relationship whereby we borrow books from parents too, making sure they are named!

Sati (4 years 5 months) loves to paint and create pictures. Her parents do not want her to do this inside the house, so they have bought her a small table and they allow her to paint outside. Her mother asked her key person if she knows of any paints that are not too messy and the practitioner was able to share with Sati's mother some ideas of how to support Sati's creativity inside as well as outside. Ideas shared included using a plastic sheet as a splash mat under  her table inside, using brushes rather than hands and fingers to paint, using a watercolour palette with blocks of colour rather than liquid paint, choosing resources that use water to draw and paint, using moon sand and using chalks and oil pastels. Sati loved bringing in her pictures to the setting and sharing with her key person the things she had created.

Hard to reach parents and hard to reach schools

Another frequently used phrase is 'hard to reach' parents. What does this phrase mean and to whom does it refer? Often this term is used when we refer to parents who do not get involved with our settings. Perhaps we have held an open evening or parent's information session and no matter what incentives we use, there always seems to be a group of parents who do not attend. Sometimes these parents can be categorised into groups such as low income, unemployed or those with EAL, however different areas will engage with different sets of parents and each area may have a unique set of 'hard to reach' parents. It is also important to note the way we view these groups, as thinking about them as 'non responsive' implies the responsibility lies fully with the parent to respond, whereas as Professor Alma Harris and Dr Janet Goodall[11] point out, 'Some "hard to reach" parents felt the school itself was indeed hard to reach.'

I would like to propose that thinking about 'hard to reach' parents is looking at it the wrong way. If a school or setting is trying to engage with parents and finds this difficult, they need to shift their thinking and ask themselves, 'Are we a hard to reach place? How can we make it easier for parents to engage with us?' Perhaps we need to redefine 'hard to reach parents' as 'hard to reach provision', turning it on its head, and if parents won't come to us, go to them. Turning the thinking on its head in this way is a proactive way of approaching the issue. It changes the source of the 'problem' from being the parents to us in the setting or school.

Aleema (4 years 9 months) lives with her mother, father, two younger siblings and her paternal grandparents in a high rise flat in London. Her family were refugees from Afghanistan and her father and grandparents have been living in the UK for nearly 17 years. Her mother moved to the UK when she married her father six years ago. Her father and grandfather speak Pashto and English, however her mother, grandmother and siblings speak mainly Pashto with a few words of English. Aleema has not attended a preschool or nursery setting but they are a sociable family who visit friends and relatives frequently so Aleema and her siblings have had plenty of opportunities to play with other children. Aleema's parents have arranged for her to start at the local Primary school. Aleema did not manage to attend the settling in sessions she was invited to and her parents did not attend the parents' information evening.

Aleema and her family could be deemed as 'hard to reach' because of cultural or language barriers and not attending school events. This particular school works hard to make itself accessible to families like Aleema's and liaises with other organisations and community projects which are set up to support such families. These are some of the strategies that the school employed to support Aleema and her family as she began school:

- The teacher and teaching assistant arranged a home visit.

- Aleema was offered additional sessions to visit school at a time when her younger siblings could also attend with her.

- Key school documents were translated into Pashto, including the school website.

- The family were put in touch with other Afghan families with older school children whose home language is Pashto.

- The family were given information about free online English classes (ESOL[12]).

- The family were offered information about a local refugee community organisation which offers practical support for families.

- School staff tried to be as sensitive as possible to the cultural needs of the family and only asked for essential information as they were aware that the family valued their privacy.

Engaging families and making our provision more accessible does not mean treating every family the same; it sometimes means the opposite. We must ensure we respect differences, celebrate similarities and try to engage with parents where they are and predominantly on their terms, whilst keeping the needs of the child paramount. This will only happen where we have fostered relationships based on mutual respect and trust.

School readiness guidance for parents

The PACEY report,[13] mentioned in Chapter 1, asked parents, 'What do you think would improve children's school readiness?' and found that most parents wanted better guidance on how to prepare children for school, more communication between parents and school, better resources to help parents and also more free-entitlement hours. We may not be able to increase the hours that their children attend our settings, but we can provide parents with more guidance, information and resources and strengthen communication links.

There is no consensus on the definition of school readiness within the early years sector, which makes it even harder for parents to understand what we mean when we use this term. We must clearly state our expectations about what we hope children can do when they start school and also be clear about what we are not expecting. Many parents may think that schools want children to know their letters and numbers or to be able to write their name. If this is not what we expect, explain to parents that this is not a prerequisite for YR and we would prefer them to be able to take themselves to the toilet independently, for example. One idea is to hold information sessions for parents so that they can hear first hand what is expected. We can offer a brief handout for parents to take home written in plain English/ other languages if appropriate, or provide something like the worksheets found in Appendix A. We can also include information about behavioural expectations as this reinforces a shared understanding of acceptable behaviour.

When Freddie (4 years 6 months) started in YR his behaviour was difficult to deal with. He shouted and screamed frequently and would find it difficult to play alongside others. His teacher noticed that he was taking the blue toys and resources away from the other children. Freddie lived at home with his mother, father, two younger brothers and one older half-sister.

Freddie's teacher built up a relationship with his mother and asked her about his preference for blue things. His mother replied that she had found it difficult to encourage her children to share so she had colour coded plates, cups and even toys at home. Blue was Freddie's colour, which explained why he believed that everything blue belonged to him. His teacher was able to work alongside the family to introduce ideas about how to share, including the problem solving approach (see Chapter 9) and was able to support Freddie to understand that colours were for everyone. Unlearning something is a difficult process and takes time. We must work closely with parents to ensure that the messages they are imparting to their children are the messages that will support them in school.

There are many ways that we can engage parents and maintain their interest in their children's learning:

- Communicate frequently with parents to keep them up to date with news and events in a variety of ways and ask them their preferences, for example face to face, letter, social media, emails, phone calls, newsletters, website.

- Identify gaps in support for particular groups of parents, for example fathers, lone parents, working parents.

- Have an open door policy, meaning that parents are welcome in at any time, and adhere to this.

- Offer workshops for parents on a variety of topics. The take up of such workshops is not always huge, but very beneficial for the parents who do attend.

- Hold regular meetings with parents and invite them to stay and play frequently.

- Set up opportunities for parents to share ideas and practical tips with other parents, for instance coffee mornings.

- Provide simple information leaflets, if possible jointly written by setting and school staff, which explain to parents expectations on entry to YR.

- Signpost parents to other support available locally, or example family support or health visitor regarding sleep issues or eating concerns.

- Share with parents the CoEL and how their child learns best.

IDEAS FOR PARENTS' WORKSHOPS

- Transition events – covering preparing your child and what to expect at school.

- Communication and Language – *chatterboxes*, *Bookstart*, rhyme sessions, play and language sessions.

- Positive change courses on routines and supporting home learning.

- Home learning programmes aiming to build parents' confidence to support learning.

- Physical Development – gym sessions, movement games, improving gross motor control.

- Promoting positive behaviour courses supporting consistency between home and settings.

In late spring, once school places had been confirmed, several settings introduced parents of children going on to the same school to each other. One preschool encouraged parents to meet informally, setting a date for a picnic in the local park and one nursery school arranged for coffee mornings for each school cohort, so that the children could play together while the parents chatted over a coffee. Another school invited parents to come and play with their children during an open session during the year prior to starting in YR. During this time staff were able to role model to parents ways of engaging with children and how to support and extend learning. They created a 'We Are Learning To' display and also created signs which they placed around the room explaining what children are learning through the various activities offered. For example, this sign about stories and rhymes was placed in the book corner (see Figure 10.1).

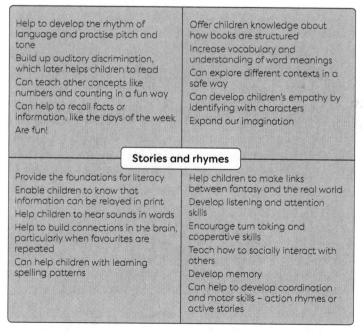

Figure 10.1 What are children learning through stories and rhymes?

For some parents school was not a happy place and memories relating to strong negative emotional responses are easy to recall. One parent told me that she does not have any happy memories of her school. Imagine what it must be like to entrust the person who is the most precious in the world to you to this place! A few weeks into the first term, one parent told a Reception class teacher, 'I was really frightened of you when my son joined your class, but now I know you are not scary at all!'

Knowing our local families and communities will go a long way in terms of supporting their children when they start school. For example, do parents take their children to the park, or local toddler group? Is there a space where parents meet and let their children play? Is there a culture of attitudes to school which are anti-establishment or fearful of authority? It is important to remember that we cannot always change the attitudes of parents in our locality, but we can change our own attitudes.

Some local authorities and boroughs have developed school readiness information for parents. Because there is no national definition, they all have slightly different takes on what school readiness means and how parents can support their children. In my opinion, the more play based and less formal the better; for example the three leaflets that Harlow Council[14] has developed focus on learning through play. Other settings have created their own leaflets aimed at parents. One school had identified a proportion of parents that were unable to read, or read English, and decided to create a poster outlining their expectations for children on entry using pictures. Another school asked me to create a leaflet aimed at parents which talks about good learners based on the CoEL as an alternative to stating specific expectations for entry to school (see Figure 10.2).

Is my child ready for school?

Within early years we often talk about how children learn and how they can become good learners.

Good learners play and explore and get engaged with activities. It's about:

Finding out and exploring – showing curiosity and interest in things, using their senses and playing with open-ended materials like cardboard boxes and large pieces of material.

Playing with what they know – pretending and role-playing, like using a wooden brick as a mobile phone, or dressing up as a pirate or doctor or fairy! It's using their imagination or telling stories.

Being willing to 'have a go' – when children have a 'can do' attitude and learn through trial and error. It's when they want to be independent, including challenging themselves and taking some risks. Having a go at climbing a tree or balancing on a wall.

Good learners are motivated to learn. It's about:

Being involved and concentrating – concentrating on something they have chosen to do and not being easily distracted. It's when they are fascinated by things and pay attention to detail, they might even concentrate so hard that they stick their tongue out!

Keeping trying – persevering and persisting even if something is difficult. Perhaps they might change the way they do something to try a different approach, like when a jigsaw piece doesn't fit one way, they turn it round.

Enjoying achieving what they set out to do – being proud of what they have achieved. Showing you their pictures and models or asking you to watch them balance or climb.

Good learners are creative and think critically. It's about:

Having their own ideas – thinking of what to do and how to do it. Finding new ways to do something or how to solve a problem like when a puzzle piece doesn't fit in the space.

Making links – noticing patterns all around them, like 'there's a cup like ours' or making predictions about what might happen, 'if we put that brick on top it will topple over' and cause and effect, 'if I press this button, something happens...'

Choosing ways to do things – deciding for themselves how to do something and thinking about what to do. It's also when children review what they have done or realise something didn't work very well and think about how to improve it next time.

Figure 10.2 An example of a leaflet for parents

A playgroup in East London in an area of deprivation where many children arrive achieving below age-related expectations, wanted to improve outcomes for children as they progress on to school. They contacted local schools to find out what they wanted in terms of their expectations for children and then developed a project with practitioners and parents engaging in activities with the children. The sorts of activities ranged from children dressing and undressing independently to visiting the local schools together. Feedback from the project was very positive, including feedback from Ofsted. The children involved in this project moved onto school achieving or exceeding age-related expectations.

The success of this project was due to the strong relationships that the setting had created with parents, which enabled them to jointly engage in activities with the children. They offered parents ideas and role modelled strategies which enhanced children's learning and parents were valued in the process.

We can suggest many ideas that will help parents to support their children prior to starting school, remembering that the most popular ideas are easy to do and free! It can be helpful if we outline what children are learning through these activities and reinforce the idea that we can all learn through play. The following list is not exhaustive but offers an example of the sort of ideas that settings were encouraging their parents to participate in:

- Take your child to the park or local playground.

- Talk to your child about what you are doing and why.

- Show an interest in what they are playing with and talk to your children about their interests.

- Encourage them to use a knife, fork, spoon and open cup whilst eating and drinking.

- Take your child to the library and borrow some books.

- Read to them at home or retell stories you remember from your childhood.

- Collect empty food packets and encourage your child to create or build with them.

- Encourage your child to draw, paint, colour and make marks on paper and card.

- Help them to learn to scoot or ride a bike or trike.

- Encourage your child to dress and undress without your help.

- Take your child to a stay and play session or toddler group.

- Make a natural collection of sticks, stones, leaves, feathers, and so on.

- Sing songs and rhymes together.

- Count steps together whilst walking up and down.

- Play catch or football or engage in sports together.

- Visit a local museum and talk about what you see there.

- Encourage children to ask questions and do your best to answer their questions honestly and at a level they will understand.

- Encourage your child to run, jump, skip, roll and climb.

- Allow them to help you with basic chores around the house and garden, for example washing up, cleaning and sorting washing.

When asked, 'How can your mummy and daddy help you to learn?' some of the children I chatted with, understandably, found this question tricky, however, others came up with a few ideas. I have recorded them verbatim to capture their thoughts as accurately as possible:

- Telling me how a baby gets out of a tummy.

- By helping me.

- By making you go to school every day even if you don't want to.

- Letting me ask questions.

- Do the same quiz at different times so I can get different scores then sometimes I might get all of them right.

- They can tell you the things that you didn't understand with the teachers.

- Help me with my spellings and give me the books too.

Yet again, the children have been very insightful and fabulously reflected upon their learning! Let's engage with parents as meaningfully as possible so that children will be supported to gain the dispositions and attitudes that underpin their success at school.

REFLECTIVE PRACTICE QUESTIONS

1. In what ways do you meaningfully engage with parents, carers and those with parental responsibility for the children in your care?

2. Are there any ways that you could be viewed as 'hard to reach provision'? What can you do about it?

3. Are parents aware of the local expectations placed on their children on entry to school? How do you know?

Notes

1. Rumbold, A. (1990) *Starting with Quality*. London: HMSO. Retrieved from www.educationengland.org.uk/documents/rumbold/rumbold1990.html, on 9 October 2017.
2. Goodall, J. and Montgomery, C. (2014) 'Parental involvement to parental engagement: a continuum.' *Educational Review*, 66(4), 399–410.
3. Siraj-Blatchford, I. and Taggart, B. (eds) (2010) *Early Childhood Matters: Evidence from the Effective Pre-school and Primary Education Project*. Abingdon: Routledge.
4. Retrieved from https://en.oxforddictionaries.com/definition/involve, on 9 October 2017.
5. Retrieved from https://en.oxforddictionaries.com/definition/engage, on 9 October 2017.
6. Goodall and Montgomery (2014), p.399.
7. Desforges, C. and Abouchaar, A. (2003) *The Impact of Parental Involvement, Parental Support and Family Education on Pupil Achievement and Adjustment: A Literature Review*. London: DfES.
8. Hunt, S., Virgo, S., Klett-Davies, M., Page, A. and Apps, J. (2010) *Provider Influence on the Early Home Learning Environment (EHLE)*. London: Department for Children, Schools and Families (DCSF).
9. Hunt *et al.* (2010).
10. Hunt *et al.* (2010).
11. Harris, A. and Goodall, J. (2008) 'Do parents know they matter? Engaging all parents in learning.' *Educational Research*, 50(3), 284.
12. See https://www.esolcourses.com.
13. Professional Association for Childcare and Early Years (PACEY) (2013) *What does "school ready" really mean?* Retrieved from https://www.pacey.org.uk/Pacey/media/Website-files/school%20ready/School-Ready-Report.pdf, on 9 October 2017, p.1.
14. Harlow Council (2017) *Is your Child Ready for School?* Retrieved from www.harlow.gov.uk/school-readiness, on 9 October 2017.

What Next? Creating Lifelong Learners

CHAPTER OBJECTIVE

This chapter will sum up, focusing in on children and how they learn. It will reiterate the key messages shared earlier in the book by summarising them and will look towards the future.

With no official definition of school readiness in the UK practitioners are left to fend for themselves when it comes to preparing children for school. There is often debate when discussing the term as school readiness links closely to the controversial formalisation of early childhood education agenda. It is vital that we keep children at the heart of all we do to ensure that they are present in this debate.

Over the years there have been several research projects looking into successful transitions and the keys to managing transitions within education.[1] Some have looked specifically at the first main transition into schools at entry.[2] Starting school is not a standardised process and there are huge variations between the experiences of children depending on where they live, their cultural background and many other variables as discussed in Chapter 2. When children begin in YR not only are the physical surroundings unfamiliar to them, but children also experience a difference in expectations from adults, new words and language and several social difficulties related to being in a large group, perhaps for the first time. Margetts and Kienig[3] point out that families are very vulnerable during this phase and we need to ensure that children have a say in the many decisions that affect them.

Transition into school is also difficult for early years practitioners and parents alike as they support children: 'the challenge is to provide a transition that stimulates growth and development while avoiding any risk of regression or failure'.[4] Thus children need to be cultivated in an environment which will enable them to thrive emotionally, physically and cognitively, which sows the seeds of creativity, thinking, exploration and imagination. They deserve nothing less.

A colleague of mine, Kym Scott,[5] has recently returned from Finland and shared a super quote from a young boy she met there in the Franzenia Childcare Centre, Helsinki. When told that most children in England start school aged four, Elliot (6 years) replied, 'That's crazy! If you start school when you're four you don't know all you need to know. You won't be ready. You haven't been born for long enough!' Elliot has summarised what many early years practitioners and teachers in Primary schools think: attending any formal education at four years old is too much too soon.[6]

This book has considered the difficulties relating to defining school readiness (Chapter 1), the many issues that affect children starting school (Chapter 2) and how focusing on the CoEL will help children to be ready to learn (Chapters 3 to 6). We have reflected upon children who are ready (Chapter 7), children-ready schools (Chapter 8), settings that support children effectively (Chapter 9) and the importance of engaging parents and carers (Chapter 10). The following summarises the points made in Chapters 7 to 10.

In summary

For children to become school ready we must:

- focus on fostering the CoEL, tapping into their interests and fascinations

- prioritise the Prime Areas and use a play-based approach

- consider developmental readiness according to the age and stage of development of each child

- ensure that early intervention takes priority in our settings

- support children through change and transitions

- encourage growth mindsets in our children

- keep children present in our thinking, listen to their views and involve them in decision making.

For schools to become child ready we must:

- gather as much information about the children as possible prior to starting and use this to tap into their interests and fascinations

- carefully consider our entry arrangements, include home visits, school visits over time, staggered entry in the autumn and smaller groups with more adult support

- provide information to settings and families about our expectations of children on entry
- build positive relationships with the children and families, identify the children's key person quickly, providing photo books to support
- build strong relationships with feeder settings, inviting them to attend school events and visiting the settings throughout the year
- create a stimulating and engaging learning environment which draws children in, captivates their interest and allows plenty of time for playing and exploring and active learning
- introduce school routines gradually over the year to the children ensuring that we go at their pace.

For settings to support children we must:

- become an active observer, identifying children's interests and fascinations and use this information to plan interesting, exciting and engaging learning opportunities
- engage in Sustained Shared Thinking with children to move their play forward, model the CoEL ourselves, scaffold activities and enhance the experience for the child
- know our children well and treat them according to their individual needs and interests
- provide an enabling environment where children can explore, investigate and experiment, allowing plenty of time for playing and exploring and active learning
- support children to be independent learners, use the problem solving approach to manage conflicts and foster the CoEL

- work collaboratively with the schools that we feed to ensure a smooth transition for the children in our care

- provide accurate assessment information about the children moving on to school.

To engage parents effectively we must:

- review our practice relating to how we engage and involve parents

- ensure that we are not a hard to reach provision

- focus on the needs of the children and signpost parents to additional support if appropriate

- provide parents with ideas for home learning opportunities

- ensure that we communicate frequently and keep parents up to date

- offer parents guidance and information relating to their child starting school, perhaps offering workshops to attend

- share with parents the CoEL and how their child learns best.

In conclusion

We need to reconsider our thoughts with regard to early childhood and starting school. Rather than the focus primarily being on school, when to start school and school readiness, perhaps we should focus more on children, what is best for young children and being ready to learn. According to Margetts and Kienig[7] there needs to be:

> [a] strong focus on the need to prepare children for school, to support them in their adjustment to school and more recently to advocate the need for schools to change their practices to be 'child ready' so that the changes children need to make to accommodate new experiences are better matched by practices in the new school.

Therefore, society needs to redefine 'readiness for school' and think about the dispositions and attitudes that will enable children to grow up to be confident, self-assured and open-minded thinkers. I believe that the CoEL are the key to developing these and the focus could be much more about readiness for learning and readiness for life.

All children are born eager to learn and this appears to be an innate quality; however, they may not be ready to learn the way that many schools teach. Winston Churchill is famously believed to have said, 'I am always ready to learn, although I do not always like being taught.' We must ensure that we are considering ways that children learn best when teaching our youngest children. They are the future of our society and world and we must instil in them the qualities that will make a better future for us all.

Whether the government in the UK takes into account the wealth of research which implies a later start to school and a delay in more formal learning benefits children remains to be seen. Schools must take note of the research, be brave enough to stand up to policy-makers and place children firmly at the centre of their policy and practice. Whether or not children are ready for school, school will loom on the horizon all too soon in the child's life. Children are not being prepared for school but prepared for life.

In fact, Kathryn Peckham[8] calls this lifelong learning, so we are laying the foundations for lifelong learning and must get it right.

I have tried to ensure that children remained central to this book, so the last word goes to Becky (5 years), who had been discussing water in great detail and stated, 'I know it in my head. I thinked it!' So let's give children the opportunity to play, explore, be creative and think to their hearts' content and our children will be ready for learning.

REFLECTIVE PRACTICE QUESTIONS

1. In the light of the whole school readiness agenda what can I do to support children and families?

2. How can I make my views known to policy-makers and decision-makers?

3. How can I ensure that children remain central to my practice?

Notes

1. Fabian, H. (2013) 'Towards Successful Transitions.' In K. Margetts and A. Kienig (eds) *International Perspectives on Transition to School: Reconceptualising Beliefs, Policy and Practice.* Abingdon: Routledge.
2. Fabian, H. (2002) *Children Starting School: A Guide to Successful Transitions and Transfers for Teachers and Assistants.* London: David Fulton Publishers.
3. Margetts, K. and Kienig, A. (2013) 'A Conceptual Framework for Transition.' In K. Margetts and A. Kienig (eds) *International Perspectives on Transition to School: Reconceptualising Beliefs, Policy and Practice.* Abingdon: Routledge, p.9.
4. Siraj-Baltchford, I. (2010) 'A Focus on Pedagogy: Case Studies of Effective Practice.' In K. Silva, E. Melhuish, P. Sammons, I. Siraj-Blatchford and B. Taggart (eds) *Early Childhood Matters Evidence from the Effective Pre-school and Primary Education Project.* Abingdon: Routledge, p.153.
5. See www.kymscottconsultancy.com
6. House, R. (2011) *Too Much, Too Soon? Early Learning and the Erosion of Childhood.* Stroud: Hawthorn Press.
7. Margetts and Kienig (2013), p.9.
8. Peckham, K. (2017) *Developing School Readiness: Creating Lifelong Learners.* London: Sage.

Appendices B–D are available to download and print from www.jkp.com/voucher using the code 4X57qNjw

'I can jigsaw' and 'My Super Skills for School'

I can jigsaw

I can keep myself clean
e.g. wash my hands and blow my nose

I can ask and answer simple questions

I can feed myself
e.g. use a knife, fork and spoon

I can take turns and listen to others

I can dress myself
e.g. socks and shoes, jumpers and coats

I can say how I feel
e.g. being proud, feeling happy

I can try new things
e.g. food, messy play

I can go to the toilet by myself
e.g. wipe my bottom, flush the toilet

I am confident to ask for help

I understand the need to follow rules

I am confident to leave my grown up

I can play on my own and alongside others

I can listen to and follow simple instructions
e.g. get your shoes

I can calm myself down
e.g. when excited, upset or angry

I can join in with stories and rhymes

My Super Skills for School

Appendix B

Notes and action planning

Choose one of the self-evaluation tools: either Appendix C 'Children-ready schools' for practitioners in schools, or Appendix D 'Settings supporting children' for practitioners in settings. Meet as a team and discuss the questions then record your ideas in the table below to ensure that you translate your ideas into action.

- What are our strengths? What do we do well?

- What changes do we want to make? (Targets for future development)

- How will these changes benefit the children?

- Tasks? How will you implement these changes? What? How? Who? When?

Task	How will this be done?	Who is responsible?	When/Timescale	Resource implications

Appendix C

Children-ready schools

A self-evaluation and review of current practice supporting schools to be ready for children

Ask ourselves these questions:

- To what extent have we reflected upon our previous transition arrangements? Can our current YR children remember what was difficult about starting school and how do we address these issues?

- How do we enable new children to become familiar with our school and staff before the beginning of term?

- Can/do we undertake home visits?

- How do we ensure that our baseline assessments or entry assessments do not get in the way of relationship building and the settling in process?

- How can we create a better sense of continuity from early years settings into school?

- Do we send our feeder preschools induction information, important dates and copies of our packs aimed at parents?

- Can we invite our feeder preschools to attend school events, e.g. Reception class nativity or sports day?

- Could we undertake a joint venture, like a teddy bears picnic, for our feeder settings or parents to attend with their children?

- How do we create opportunities for children to take some control of the transition and feel involved in the process?

- How do we receive information from settings?

- Does this information answer all the questions that we have about the child – if not have we fed this back to the settings?

- How do we celebrate what each child brings with them and has learned at home and at previous settings?

- How do we acknowledge children's thoughts and feelings as part of the transition process?

- How do we take into account children's existing friendships and support them to form new ones?

- Do we have a range of books and resources to support transition, which also reflect the background and culture of the children due to start to help them to feel secure?

- Can we donate some school uniform to our feeder settings for them to use in role play?

- Have we considered the use of transitional objects and comforters in our school?

- Are adults positive role models, always displaying the behaviour we expect from children, e.g. using quiet voices, being respectful, resolving conflict, asking questions?

- Do adults promote problem solving as a response to resolving conflicts?

- Have we planned for times during the day when children could find it difficult, e.g. transitions, arrivals, lunch time, play time, going home time, staff change-over, etc.?

- Are we consistent when boundary setting within school and in partnership with parents?

- How well do we know our parents? Do they feel able to share personal details with us, e.g. changes at home?

- How well do we work with parents, engaging them in their children's learning and offering support for their learning at home?

- How strong are our links with other settings and professionals? Can we develop these links further?

- Which questions always come up at the new parents evenings? Can we pre-empt this or alleviate parents' concerns in some other way prior to the children starting school?

- Could we make any improvements to our welcome pack?

- Are there any opportunities before term starts for 1:1 conversations between parents/carers and Reception teachers?

- Is everyone clear about the school's expectations in terms of children and parents before the children start school?

- Are practical issues clearly addressed, e.g. times to drop off, where to leave the children, whether or not parents are welcome into the class, where children put coats, water bottles, book bags? Is this explained to both parents and children?

- To what extent do we ease children into school life and gradually introduce things like assemblies and play time with the older children? Do we need to review this?

Settings supporting children

Self-evaluation and review of current practice supporting children to be school ready

Ask ourselves these questions:

- How do we create opportunities for children to take some control of the transition and feel involved in the process?

- How can we create a better sense of continuity from early years settings into school?

- How is information passed on to future settings/ schools?

- Does this information answer all the questions that the future setting/school has about the child? How can we find out?

- How are children's interests reflected in the information we pass on?

- How do we acknowledge children's thoughts and feelings as part of the transition process?

- Do we have a range of books and resources to support transition which also reflect the background and culture of the children moving on to help them to feel secure?

- Do we have opportunities for children to role play at being at school?

- Could we invite children to bring in shorts and t-shirts to have a few practice PE sessions, when the children change for PE?

- Can we ask to attend school events, e.g. Reception class nativity or sports day?

- Could we undertake a joint venture, like a teddy bears picnic, with our local schools?

- Have we considered the use of transitional objects and comforters in our setting?

- Are adults positive role models, always displaying the behaviour we expect from children, e.g. using quiet voices, being respectful, resolving conflict, asking questions?

- Do adults promote problem solving as a response to resolving conflicts?

- Have we planned for times during the day when children could find it difficult, e.g. transitions, arrivals, going home time, staff change-over, etc.?

- Are we consistent when boundary setting within the setting, in partnership with parents and across all age ranges?

- How well do we know our parents? Do they feel able to share personal details with us, e.g. changes at home?

- How well do we work with parents, engaging them in their children's learning and offering support for their learning at home?

- How strong are our links with other settings, local schools and professionals?

- Have we kept local schools up to date with any changes in our setting?

- Have we reflected on how we prepare children and their parents for school?

- Could we hold a parents evening part way through the year and invite a teacher to explain about expectations from a school's point of view? This may help to alleviate the pressure to prepare children academically in some way.

- What sort of questions and concerns do parents raise about the transition to school? Can we answer their questions and alleviate their concerns?

- Are we clear about the expectations of local schools in terms of children being school ready? If not, how can we find out?

- Can we hold an information event for parents on school readiness and invite local schools to send a representative to attend?

Appendix E

Books about starting school

Adamson, Jean. *Topsy and Tim Start School* ISBN: 9781409300830

Ahlberg, Janet. *Starting School* ISBN: 9780670816880

Anholt, Laurence. *Billy and the Big New School* ISBN: 9781843625834

Barber, Nicola. *First Day at School* ISBN: 9780750265164

Barkow, Henriette. *Tom and Sofia Start School* (dual language book – available in over 27 languages) ISBN: 9781844445622

Brooks, Felicity. *Max and Millie Start School* ISBN: 9781409546030

Butterworth, Nick. *Sports Day* ISBN: 9780340932407

Child, Lauren. *I am Too Absolutely Small for School* ISBN: 9781843623663

Chichester Clark, Emma. *Come to School Too, Blue Kangaroo!* ISBN: 9780007258673

Civardi, Anne. *Going to School* ISBN: 0746066600

Cutbill, Andy. *First Week at Cow School* ISBN: 9780007274680

Guillain, Charlotte. *School for Dads* ISBN: 9781405277495

Hill, Eric. *Spot Goes to School* ISBN: 0140506500

Horse, Harry. *Little Rabbit Goes to School* ISBN: 9780670912834

Hart, Caryl. *The Wolf Who Wouldn't Go to School* (Whiffy Wilson) ISBN: 9781408325865

Hart, Caryl and Eaves, Ed. *Welcome to Alien School* (other books in this series too) ISBN: 9780857072573

Hunt, Roderick. *Starting School* ISBN: 9780198487951

Hunter, Rebecca. *My First Day at School* ISBN: 023752693X

Jenner, Caryn. *Starting School* ISBN: 9781445100944

Joyce, Melanie. *My School Peg* ISBN: 9781844226030

Latimer, Miriam. *Dear Panda* ISBN: 9781849416542

Lewis, Kim. *My Friend Harry* ISBN: 9780744552959

Northway, Jennifer. *See You Later, Mum!* ISBN: 9781847461520

Powell, Jillian. *My New School* ISBN: 9780750262842

Roc, Margaret. *Jellybean Goes to School* ISBN: 9781848530751

Thomas, Pat. *Do I Have to Go to School?* ISBN: 9780340894521

Weston, Carrie. *Boris Starts School* ISBN: 9780192758323

White, Kathryn. *Ruby's School Walk* ISBN: 9781846867866

Vulliamy, Clara. *I Heart School* (Martha and the Bunny Brothers) ISBN: 9780007419173

Whybrow, Ian. *Bella Goes to School* ISBN: 9780330509565

Whybrow, Ian. *Harry and the Dinosaurs Go to School* ISBN: 9780141502441

Glossary

The following key terms are given in italic the first time they occur in the book.

Amygdala The part of your brain that deals with stress and emotion. Think freeze, fight or flight response.

Atelierista This is the name given to the practitioner with an arts background in the municipal preschools of Reggio Emilia, Northern Italy, who works with the children in creating different projects and enhancing their creativity.

Autumn born children This refers to the time of year when a child has a birthday. If they are born between 1 September and 31 December they are autumn born. These children are the oldest in a class in England.

Bookstart This is a programme run by BookTrust, the UK's largest children's reading charity. Every child in England is currently entitled to a free Bookstart pack at 0 to 12 months and three to four years. https://www.booktrust.org.uk/supporting-you/families/our-programmes/bookstart.

Cerebrum The largest part of the brain, divided into the left and right hemispheres. This is the thinking part of the brain.

Characteristics of Effective Learning (CoEL) These are outlined in the Early Years Foundation Stage in England and refer to the different ways that children learn. Three Characteristics of Effective Learning are playing and exploring, active learning and creating and thinking critically.

Chatterboxes This is an idea to encourage children to talk about familiar things from home. They place a few toys or photographs that are special to them in a shoe box and take it into school to share with other children or adults.

Child-initiated learning This is when children take their own learning forward, following their own lines of enquiry. They might be playing within an environment that has been carefully structured and planned by an adult but the children are free to play, explore, investigate and discover at their own pace and in their own time.

Cognitive frames These are the structures in our thinking that help us to make sense of the world and complex information. Cognitive frames influence how we think, feel and behave in relation to a specific issue and can limit our thinking. For example, time frames set the deadlines within which we work.

Continuous provision When we offer free access to resources and learning opportunities to children on a daily basis – this is our continuous provision. It may include role play, mark-making, sand, water, books, dough, messy play, construction, creative area, ICT, small world, music, puzzles, etc. Effective practitioners enhance their continuous provision to keep it exciting, stimulating and interesting, linking in with the children's interests, topics, themes or core texts.

Development Matters Produced by Early Education with support from the Department for Education as a non-statutory guidance document supporting practitioners to implement the requirements of the Statutory Framework for the EYFS. https://www.early-education.org.uk/development-matters.

Differentiate When adults plan additional opportunities within an activity to meet the needs of all children, accommodating the differences between learners.

Early Learning Goals (ELGs) End of EYFS descriptors of achievement, assessed at the end of the Reception year in England.

Early Years Foundation Stage (EYFS) This is the statutory framework in England covering learning, development and care for children from birth to five. It provides seven areas of learning and development and describes the Early Learning Goals (ELGs).

Early Years Foundation Stage Profile (EYFSP) This is a summative assessment undertaken at the end of the EYFS (usually in YR). It summarises children's attainment in terms of the 17 Early Learning Goals (ELGs) and provides a short narrative in relation to the Characteristics of Effective Learning.

Ecological systems theory/bioecological model Urie Bronfenbrenner has attempted to explain the interconnectedness of children's lives and both aspects of nature and nurture through his ecological systems theory, which was later renamed the bioecological model. This is a theoretical perspective explaining how humans are affected by an interconnected system with many different parts or environments. He labelled these parts the microsystem, mesosystem, macrosystem, exosystem and later, chronosystem. They have been described as layers in an onion, nested systems or Russian dolls and focus on children's lives in terms of the processes and conditions that influence them at different times.

Emotional intelligence This refers to the ability to recognise your own and other people's feelings and emotions. Developed by Dan Goleman and others, emotional intelligence generally includes personal skills such as self-awareness, self-regulation and motivation, and social skills such as empathy, and relationship and interpersonal skills.

English as an Additional Language (EAL) These children have a home language other than English and we must give learners who speak English as an Additional Language an equal opportunity to access learning. According to the British Council there are more than a million learners with EAL in UK schools.

Enhanced provision This is when we enhance our continuous provision to keep it exciting, stimulating and interesting. It can be linked to the children's interests, topics, themes or core texts. Whenever possible it should be related to their first hand experiences, e.g. after visiting a farm practitioners placed farm animals and tractors in the digging area, created a farm shop role play area and invited children to make sheep pens and cow sheds from construction materials.

Fixed and growth mindset Carol Dweck coined the terms 'fixed' and 'growth' mindsets to describe people who believe that their intelligence, talents and abilities are just given, fixed traits (fixed) or that these talents, abilities and intelligences can be developed through hard work and education (growth). Fostering a growth mindset will enhance a child's capacity to learn.

Forest school This is a type of outdoor learning (for all ages – nursery to adult) replicating teaching in Denmark which uses the outdoor environment, specifically forests and woodland, to teach children practical skills and build their self-esteem and independence. Typically children who participate in forest school activities go out in all weathers and engage in risky play within the safe boundaries that are set by the practitioners.

Formative assessment This is the process of seeking and interpreting evidence for use by children and their practitioners to determine where the learners are in their learning, where they need to go next and how best to get there, e.g. observing children during play, thinking about what has been seen and using this knowledge to plan their next steps in their learning and development.

Good Level of Development (GLD) This term is used in relation to the Early Years Foundation Stage Profile Statutory Assessment in England. A child has achieved a GLD when they have met the end of year expectations (ELGs) in the three Prime Areas (Personal, Social and Emotional Development, Physical Development and Communication and Language) and in Literacy and Mathematics. The Government publishes the EYFSP results in terms of GLD and this is the standard often equated with school readiness in the media.

HighScope This term is now used to describe an educational approach to early years focusing on active learning, a consistent daily routine, stimulating learning environment, observational assessment and adult–child relationships. It advocates a problem solving approach to conflict resolution. Historically, HighScope began with the Perry Preschool Project which was a longitudinal research study following 123 children in Michigan in the 1960s. Some of these children followed the HighScope Curriculum and a control group did not. The researchers tracked these children into adulthood and have found huge benefits for attending a preschool HighScope programme such as being more likely to hold down a long-term relationship, less likely to commit a crime and more likely to earn more. https://highscope.org/perrypreschoolstudy

Intrinsic and extrinsic motivation Intrinsic motivation is when you do something simply because you enjoy doing it, e.g. taps into a child's interests, captures their imagination, child has fun. Extrinsic motivation is when you want to do it to gain a reward or to avoid punishment, e.g. reward charts, stickers, time out.

Learning objectives These state what children are expected to learn during a session, lesson or project.

Mosaic approach This approach attempts to include the voices of young children and listen to them using various methods in order to gain a deeper understanding of their lives.

Ofsted Ofsted is the Office for Standards in Education, Children's Services and Skills in England. It inspects and regulates services that care for children and young people.

Pedagogista This term means teacher or educator and each of the municipal preschools of Reggio Emilia, Northern Italy, has a Pedagogista and Atelierista working with the children.

PenPal electronic pen Developed by Mantra Lingua, this electronic pen will 'read' the text to you in any language it is programmed to read. It works by detecting micro bar code links on the text that are wirelessly connected to audio files in your computer. http://uk.mantralingua.com/product/penpal

Plan-do-review Sometimes referred to as Assess, Plan, Do, Review. The idea is to start with what a child can do (Assess), plan future learning opportunities or interventions (Plan), put them into place (Do), and then review their progress (Review). Children can engage in this cycle themselves by planning to do something, doing it and then reviewing their progress with an adult, which leads on to planning the next activity.

Pre-operational/concrete operational stage of cognitive development Piaget's theory of cognitive development consists of four stages; sensorimotor (birth to age 2), pre-operational stage (from age 2 to age 7), concrete operational stage (from age 7 to age 11) and formal operational stage (age 11+ – adolescence and adulthood). According to Piaget, at the pre-operational stage children learn through symbolic play, are egocentric and believe their toys and other inanimate objects are alive with feelings. At the concrete operational stage they are developing logic but still find abstract thinking difficult.

Prime Areas Within the EYFS in England there are seven areas of learning and development divided into the Prime and Specific Areas. The Prime Areas comprise of Personal, Social and Emotional Development (PSED), Physical Development (PD) and Communication and Language (CL) and are essential for healthy development and lay the foundations for future learning.

Provocations When we present resources and materials in such a way that they invite children to learn or provoke learning to take place.

Pupil Premium Previously called Free School Meals, this is the additional funding for publicly funded schools in England to help raise the attainment of disadvantaged pupils. A similar funding programme has been rolled out to early years providers called Early Years Pupil Premium.

Reception year (YR) This refers to the first year group in a Primary or Infant school. Children are received into school in England and Wales into a Reception class. Children are usually aged between four and five years old.

Scaffolding This is a bit like actual scaffolding, when a building needs support around it. In order to support children we offer them additional materials, ask questions or make suggestions to help them progress in their learning.

Schematic behaviour This is when children engage in play that is repetitive in nature such as lining up toys, filling and emptying boxes and containers and mixing materials together, or when they appear fascinated by movements of objects and how they move themselves, e.g. rolling, looking at things upside down, throwing objects and toys or moving toys from one place to another. For further reading see *Observing and Developing Schematic Behaviour in Young Children* ISBN 9781785921797.

Schoolification This term refers to the top-down pressure felt by early childhood settings to make their provision more 'school like' and formal.

Special Educational Need or Disability (SEND) Some children may have a Special Educational Need or Disability that makes it harder for them to learn than others and they may need additional help or extra support.

Specific Areas Within the EYFS in England there are seven areas of learning and development divided into the Prime and Specific Areas. The Specific Areas build on the Primary areas and consist of Literacy, Mathematics, Understanding the World and Expressive Arts and Design.

Spring born children This refers to the time of year when a child has a birthday. If they are born between 1 January and 31 March they are spring born.

Statutory/compulsory school age A child is of compulsory school age the term after their fifth birthday. For children with a birthday in the autumn or spring term this will fall during the Reception year. For summer born children this will be during the first term of Year 1 in a Primary or Infant school.

Stay and play This term usually describes sessions where parents are invited to bring their children to play and stay with them during the session. They are an opportunity to build relationships and for practitioners to model interacting with children to parents.

Success criteria This helps a teacher or pupil decide if they have met the learning objectives of the session and been successful in their learning. It shares the responsibility of learning with the children rather than the onus remaining with the teacher, e.g. if the learning objective were, 'Every child will write their name' the success criteria would be, 'I can write my name.'

Summative assessment Summative assessment is any assessment that summarises where learners are at a given point in time – it provides a snapshot of what has been learned in terms of attainment and achievement. Tick lists of achievement, tests and exams are all forms of summative assessment. However, *formative assessment* is considered to be effective practice within the early years. This is the process of observing children, thinking about what has been seen and using this knowledge to plan the next steps in their learning and development.

Summer born children This refers to the time of year when a child has a birthday. If they are born between 1 April and 31 August they are summer born. These children are the youngest in a class in England.

Sustained Shared Thinking When two or more people discuss an issue, problem or concept to extend and further develop children's thinking. This phrase arose out of the Effective Provision of Preschool Education (EPPE) research which began in 2003.

Synapses This term is used to describe the process of passing electrical or chemical signals from one neuron to another. Although they make a connection, the word connection is misleading as there is a tiny synaptic gap between the neurons over which the signals pass.

Thalamus Large mass of grey matter located in the hindbrain. The thalamus acts like an air-traffic controller processing and relaying sensory information on to different parts of the brain.

Too much too soon This is a campaign run by the Save Childhood Movement who believe that children in England are starting formal learning too early, which is damaging their long-term health and wellbeing. www.toomuchtoosoon.org

Zone of Proximal Development Vygotsky developed a concept which he named the Zone of Proximal Development. This is the difference between what a child can achieve independently and what a child can achieve with guidance and encouragement from a more knowledgeable partner. We should aim to offer children opportunities within this zone which extend their thinking and enable them to achieve more than they would have achieved alone.

Index

Hamscom, Angela 75
Harris, Alma 162
HighScope Educational Research
    Foundation 144
holistic view of school readiness
    24–7
home learning environment
    influences on 158–61
Home-Start UK 17, 21
home visits
    conducting 123–6
    importance of 122–3
    tips for successful 126–7
House, Richard 33
Huber, Mike 131
Hundred Review (Early Excellence)
    21, 34–5

idea development
    and critical thinking 88–90
independent learning
    support for 139–41
Interacting or Interfering? (Fisher) 80
international comparisons
    on start of school 38–40, 175
involvement of children in learning
    52

Key, The 21, 23, 24
Kienig, A. 174–5, 179
knowledge and understanding of
    world
    in play-based learning 64–5

Leitch, Neil 33
Letters and Sounds (DCSF) 32
lifelong learning
    preparation for 179–80

Malaguzi, Loris 99
Margetts, K. 174–5, 179
Montgomery, C. 156, 158
More Great Childcare 20
motivation
    intrinsic and extrinsic 72
    role in active learning 72–3

National Association for the
    Education of Young Children
    (NAEYC) 16–17

OECD 31, 116
Ofsted 20, 21, 22, 36–7
open-ended activities
    and play-based learning 63

Palmer, Sue 33, 34, 38
parents
    'hard to reach' 161–4
    in home learning environment
        158–61
    involvement and engagement
        differences 156–8
    school readiness guidance for
        164–72
    school's view of 158
    support as school starting factor
        43
    tips for engagement 178
perseverance
    and active learning 76–7
personalised learning
    and CoEL 53–5
Piaget, Jean 92
play-based learning
    adult role in 67–9
    assessment for 69–70
    'can do' attitude 65–6
    closed activities 63–4
    curiosity in 62–3
    and exploration 62–3
    and formal learning 32–7, 39–40
    and knowledge and
        understanding of world
        64–5
    open-ended activities 63
    planning for in CoEL 35–6
    and school readiness 67
Professional Association for
    Childcare and Early Years
    (PACEY) 16, 164

Tamsin Grimmer is an experienced consultant and trainer, a director of Linden Learning and a lecturer in Early Years at Bath Spa University. Tamsin is passionate about young children's learning and development and is fascinated by how very young children think. She believes that all children deserve practitioners who are inspiring, dynamic, reflective and passionate about teaching them and who have a keen interest in the different ways that children learn. Tamsin is particularly interested in play, schemas, active learning, promoting positive behaviour and supporting early language development. In her spare time, Tamsin is in her final year studying for a Masters Degree in Early Childhood Education at the University of Chester.